SOCIALISM AND COMMUNISM

IN

THEIR PRACTICAL APPLICATION.

AMS PRESS

NEW YORK

SOCIALISM AND COMMUNISM

IN

THEIR PRACTICAL APPLICATION.

BY THE

REV. M. KAUFMANN, M.A.

Author of " Socialism : its Nature, its Dangers, and its Remedies ; "
" Utopias ; or, Schemes of Social Improvement, from Sir Thomas More to
Karl Marx," &c., &c.

———◇◆◇———

PUBLISHED UNDER THE DIRECTION OF THE COMMITTEE OF GENERAL
LITERATURE AND EDUCATION APPOINTED BY THE SOCIETY
FOR PROMOTING CHRISTIAN KNOWLEDGE.

———◇◆◇———

LONDON:

SOCIETY FOR PROMOTING CHRISTIAN KNOWLEDGE,
NORTHUMBERLAND AVENUE, CHARING CROSS, W.C.;
43, QUEEN VICTORIA STREET, E.C.;
26, ST. GEORGE'S PLACE, HYDE PARK CORNER, S.W.
BRIGHTON: 135, NORTH STREET.
NEW YORK: E. & J. B. YOUNG & CO.

1883.

Reprinted from the edition of 1883, London
First AMS edition published 1971
Manufactured in the United States of America

International Standard Book Number: 0-404-08447-8

Library of Congress Catalog Card Number: 76-134403

AMS PRESS INC.
NEW YORK, N. Y. 10003

CONTENTS.

		PAGE
CHAPTER I.	Communism of the Early Christians	5
II.	Common life in the Middle Ages	23
III.	Pre-Reformation Socialisms	46
IV.	The Hussites and the Peasants' War	68
V.	The Moravian Brotherhood	91
VI.	The Christian Republic at Paraguay	117
VII.	Communistic Societies in America, I.	145
VIII.	Communistic Societies in America, II	163
IX.	Old Mortality of Socialism	179
X.	"Social Palaces"	203
XI.	"Colleges of Industry"	235

SOCIALISM AND COMMUNISM.

CHAPTER I.

COMMUNISM OF THE EARLY CHRISTIANS.

IN the present work we propose to examine some of the most important experiments, made from time to time by social reformers, to realise in actual life their theories of social improvement. We shall pass in review the various Communistic attempts to introduce more simple forms of life, and to bring about a greater equality of fortune and happiness,—in short, "fraternal union among men for industrial purposes, a working in common for the common good."

In doing so we shall have occasion to point out how far the theory and practice agree, and to what extent the societies so formed differ from and fall short of the ideals of the writers of Utopias.

Remembering the ancient adage, *experientia*

docet (experience teaches), we shall be able from
the results obtained to draw our conclusions as
to the feasibility or impracticability of Socialistic theories, and thus have it in our power,
from a review of Communistic societies, past and
present, to supply the materials for a critique
on the theory of Socialism and Communism
generally. We shall begin with the social principles of the early Christians and the Essenes,
and then proceed to trace the history of later
Communisms down to the present day.

Communistic societies existed before the
Christian era, but under totally different circumstances. The Cretans and the Spartans,
for example, possessed such institutions. Madame Roland, a fervent admirer and a victim
of the French Revolution, even shed tears
because she was not destined to live in Sparta
at a time when these institutions existed
there. But the equality practised in Sparta
was only an equality of *free* citizens. Slaves
had to do the greater share of the work in the
State, without being allowed to participate in
the privileges of citizenship. When Christianity
" gave a new turn to the life of our race," by
the abolition of slavery,—which was one of the
most startling of its indirect results,—it set up
a principle which placed the bondman and the
freeman on a social level. The moral enthusiasm

which springs from religious convictions is a
prime motor in all social reform, and hence there
came into action a powerful influence on European society as Christianity gradually spread
throughout the Roman Empire.   The effects of
this movement on the history of the world
were so peculiar and distinct from all that had
preceded it that we may well confine ourselves,
in our review of Communistic societies, to such
as have since been founded.

It has been pointed out again and again that
when Christianity first appeared in the Roman
Empire that Empire was torn asunder by social
class divisions; great distress and despair existed among the masses of the people, and the
new religion was naturally regarded "as the
ideal of popular hope and longing," holding out
as it did the promise of "an immense renovation
and transformation of things."

The gulf between rich and poor—a small
minority monopolising all the wealth of the
empire, whilst the people were living in abject
poverty — threatened to bring about a serious
social disruption.   As a matter of fact, for
several centuries before the birth of Christ social
questions were occupying the minds of the
people, and their discussion was gradually leading to the destruction of the Roman Empire.
A hundred years before Christ all the property

of the city of Rome was shared by 2,000 families, "the magnates of birth and commerce." The remainder of the population consisted of poor freemen, to the number of a million and a quarter, mainly paupers depending for their livelihood on public largesses, while probably forty in every hundred were slaves. The ownership of land was confined to a small number of proprietors, and the soil was cultivated by bands of slaves, who were often treated most cruelly by their masters. The class of small farmers, no longer able to enter into competition with the owners of vast lands, disappeared, and their holdings became the pleasure-gardens of the rich purchasers. Usury and mercantile speculation spread ruin among all but the great capitalists. Referring to the dependencies and colonies, the Roman satirist remarks, " We devour nations to the very sinews." The farmers and collectors of taxes, on account of their rapacity, became the most hated class of Roman officials. The wealth extorted from the provinces increased the chasm between a bloated plutocracy and the impoverished proletarians [1]

[1] *Proletarians*, French *prolétaire*, the lowest and poorest class in the community. The word is derived from the Latin *proletarii*, the name given in the census of Servius Tullius to the lowest of the *centuries*, or subdivisions of citizens, to indicate that they were valuable to the state only as rearers of offspring (*proles*).

in the capital. A fortune of £15,000 was considered small for a senator, and the dowry of £12,500, given by Scipio Africanus to his daughter, was regarded as very insignificant. Cicero had *only* a fortune of £150,000, and the King of Cappadocia owed to Pompey alone five times that sum, whilst the landed property of Crassus was valued at £1,600,000. This enormous increase of wealth among a few led to effeminate luxury, and the expenditure of vast sums of money often on a single feast, whilst penury and privation became the lot of millions of free and slave labourers, whose destitute condition was only mitigated, and their thoughts diverted from outbreak, by dispensing among them " bread and games " (*panem et circenses*).

" A more repulsive picture can hardly be imagined," says Professor Beesly, in his description of the Roman society of the time. " A mob, a moneyed class, and an aristocracy almost equally worthless, hating each other and hated by the rest of the world. . . . Swarms of slaves beginning to brood over revenge as a solace to their sufferings ; the land going out of cultivation ; native industry swamped by slave-grant imposts ; the population decreasing ; the army degenerating ; wars waged as a speculation, but only against the weak ; provinces subjected to organised pillage ; in the metropolis, childish superstition, wholesale luxury, and monstrous vice. The hour for reform was surely come[1]."

Nothing but a radical change could save Roman society from utter ruin. Christianity appeared as a great regenerating principle to renovate the Roman world. The oppressed, the slave, the weary, and the heavy-laden found comfort in a religion that taught mankind the duty of fraternal love. The stern, hard, selfish world was arrested on its reckless course of self-indulgence by St. Paul's admonition from his Roman prison: "Look not every man on his own things, but every man also on the things of others." Christianity in teaching the Gospel to the poor changed the face of the ancient world.

In speaking, however, of the Communism of the early Christians as distinguished from its later development, it is to be remembered that the Christian Communism of the Apostolic age was *voluntary*, and the outcome of the self-denying love of the brethren, and that in this respect it differed essentially from the Communism taught at the present day, which demands an equality enforced by a central authority, and which so far from inculcating a spirit of self-denial, looks for the self-indulgence of all.

Modern Communists, with their sympathisers,

[1] A. H. Beesly, "The Gracchi, Marius, and Sulla," p. 21.

affirm that Communism was the natural outcome of the Law of Equality implied in Christ's
teaching [1]. That the principle did not hold its
ground is ascribed by them to the ambition and
worldliness of the Church as she increased in
power, especially after her official recognition
as the State religion of the Roman Empire.
After this alliance with wealth and grandeur,
they say the Church rapidly departed from the
simplicity of the gospel, and consoled herself by
the acquisition of temporal aggrandisement for
her disappointment in not attaining to the long-
deferred hope of a final "restitution of all
things."

On the other hand, the defenders of the principle of individual property as opposed to Communism (which in their opinion is "a mutiny
against society") deny that the Church ever
sanctioned officially, or that her Founder ever
recommended, such a custom as that of "having
all things in common."

As a matter of fact we may say, with an
able Church historian, that "the community in
Jerusalem growing out of the Society of the
Apostles, who were accustomed already to the
common-purse system, hit upon the daring plan

[1] "Jesus Christ Himself not only proclaimed, preached,
and prescribed Communism as a consequence of fraternity,
but practised it with His apostles."—Cabet, "Voyage en
Icarie," p. 567.

of establishing a community of goods. And this was fostered by the first outburst of enthusiastic brotherly love, being all the more readily accepted in consequence of the prevailing expectation among the disciples of the approaching subversion of all things."

According to this explanation the Communism practised by the early Church was not so much a rigid logical deduction from the teaching of Christ as it was the result of spontaneous " Love of the Brethren," who were all united by the same common bond, and all equally ready to devote their goods and possessions to the common welfare.

One great idea was ever before the minds of this small band of early Christians, that the great coming catastrophe, " the end of all things," was at hand. Property and position, and indeed all worldly matters, were consequently regarded by them as of secondary importance on the eve of such a momentous crisis.

The Master Himself had left no definite instructions as to the future social organisation of His " little flock." It had been His plan all along to lay down general principles, leaving them to be worked out in the course of time, rather than to prescribe definite lines of conduct under given circumstances. His kingdom was not of this world. He left no political creed for His followers. During His ministerial life He had shown His deep sympathy with the poor and oppressed; but He had never encouraged them to better their condition by social revolutions. He recognised the existing state of things, and tolerated the unsatisfactory condition of society, not, however, without pointing to the root of the evil. He expressed His abhorrence of the degeneracy of the times, and attacked in terms of withering indignation the class-pride of the wealthy and privileged sections of society. The ideal of a perfect society was ever held up by Him to His most intimate disciples. He formed no plan, however, for realising this ideal in an ecclesiastical polity. The working out of His principles was left to the "new leaven," which was to reform character, and thus indirectly *society*.

The "sacredness of the money-bag," as the Socialist Lassalle sneeringly calls it, is not upheld in the gospel. On the contrary, wealth and pomp are regarded with contempt as compared with "the pearl of great price." On the other hand, the "patrimony of the poor" is not to be restored by means of Social reform, but gradually by moral influences which would bring about a tendency towards better things. In the meanwhile the rich are to bridge over the gulf between Dives and Lazarus by supplying from

their own superfluities the needs of the destitute. "If thou wilt be perfect," says Jesus
to the well-disposed young man of property,
"go and sell all that thou hast, and give to the
poor, and thou shalt have treasure in heaven"
(St. Matthew xix. 21). The sanctity and dignity of labour as a duty, of the highest as well
as of the lowest, is also indirectly enforced by
the example of Christ Himself, who before His
public ministry was engaged in industrial work.

In all this we see His sympathy with *all*
classes, and can observe the correcting influences
of a new and spiritual religious system introduced by one who fully comprehended the needs
of His own age, and cautiously applied the
remedies of His own Divine *Therapeutics* to
individuals here and there, in preference to pro-
pounding revolutionary theories for the reconstruction of society.

It is not from the great Master, then, that
the Communistic scheme of the early Church
was derived, although we cannot help avowing
that there was nothing either in His teaching
or practice to discourage its adoption.

What, then, gave the first impulse to a
system introduced by the disciples without the
express command of their Lord, and soon discontinued when its impracticability was discovered? We have already expressed the opinion

that the practice in question originated in the common-purse system prevailing among the disciples during our Lord's ministry, a practice that after His departure was further extended. We may add that perhaps its introduction was facilitated by the influence of a body of religious mystics tolerably well known at the time, the Essenes.

It is almost certain, that this Jewish sect of ascetics was not in any way historically connected with the Apostolic Church. Still there were some points of contact between the two. The high moral standard of the Essenes, their Puritanical contempt of this world, their monastic rigour in the pursuit of godliness, and their love of contemplative seclusion, would naturally attract the attention and gain the respect of the early Christians. There is, therefore, no great improbability in the supposition that the organisation of the Christian Church was more or less influenced by the modes of social life peculiar to this fraternity.

Theoretically, according to Philo, the Essenes regulated their conduct by these three injunctions : *Love God, love virtue, love mankind.* Practically, like the early Christians, they despised wealth, and considered vows of poverty to be acceptable to God. " It is a law among them," says Josephus, " that those who come to them *must let what they have be common* to the whole order, insomuch—that among them all there is no appearance of poverty or excess of riches, but every one's possessions are inter-mingled with every other's possessions; and so there is, as it were, *one patrimony among all the brethren* [1]."

There is nothing improbable in the conjecture that the early Christians were moved by such views, nor is it in any way derogatory to the prestige of the early Church that it should have been influenced in this matter by the least corrupt and most respectable among God's ancient people.

Self-renunciation and simple forms of life were the leading tenets both of the Essenes and the Hebrew Christians, and the latter accordingly adopted a similar, if not identical, social polity.

In other respects the early Christians differed

[1] Josephus (*Jew. War*, Bk. ii. ch. 8) says that there were three philosophical sects among the Jews, viz. the Pharisees, the Sadducees, and the Essenes. As modern writers have however pointed out, the Pharisees formed the great mass of the nation, while the Sadducees were merely a political party who did not accept the traditions of their adversaries. The Essenes were, as far as is known, a very small body—never numbering over 4,000. Josephus gives an extremely flat-tering account of them, which is, however, regarded by many modern inquirers as similar to the account given by Tacitus in his *Germania* of the German tribes of his day. The Essenes, who were certainly the strictest of all Jews, had for their motto, " Mine is thine, and thine is mine."

from the Essenes, but to them of the existing Jewish sects the Church of Jerusalem most naturally inclined in adopting the theory and practice of communistic life.

The experiment was tried of establishing a " Commonwealth of Love." After an ephemeral existence the attempt had to be abandoned, just as the ideals of our youth are often shattered by the stern realities of riper experience.

But although " this first heroic effort against selfishness," and endeavour to remodel society on a simple basis, proved vain, the idea of a thorough social reformation in the Church, and by the Church, was not lost sight of, but has been cherished ever since by devout and noble souls at different periods of Church history. We have glimpses of it in the early Fathers (to which allusion will be made further on); and it has found a full expression in the con- stitution of the monastic orders and heretical sects, founded during the middle ages. It was again revived during the stormy periods of the Reformation and the Revolution, and is being carried into effect at this very moment in a modified form among the Moravians, and almost literally among those transatlantic, semi-reli- gious Communistic societies described in a recently published volume of Mr. Nordhoff.

M. Renan supplies a reason for this recurrence

c

to the social pattern of the early Christian community, notwithstanding so many baffled trials and crushing disappointments. He holds that the wants represented in the first attempt of the Church to establish Communism are lasting, and he even ventures to predict the final realisation of the idea itself. " The psalm, ' Behold how good and joyful a thing it is, brethren, to dwell together in unity ! ' has ceased to be ours. But when modern individualism has borne its last fruits ; when humanity, dwarfed, dismal, impuissant, shall return to great institutions and their strong discipline ; when our paltry shop-keeping society—I say rather, when our world of pigmies—shall have been driven out with scourges by the heroic and idealistic portions of humanity—then *life in common* will be realised again."

We feel that after all we have here only a reiteration of the same undefined longings and yearnings of our common humanity, a seeking after that something which in the moments of our unselfish (some will say unthinking) reveries we muse over, but which in the calmer hours of rational reflection we know to be only a delightful dream. For so long at least as human beings continue to be constituted as they are, and the struggle for existence remains the rule of life, a hope of universal equality must continue to be a poetic fancy, and the ideal of a perfect society on Communistic principles an unattainable aspiration.

We have seen that the Communism of the early Christians was the result of religious ardour, the first-fruits, so to speak, of the newly embraced faith manifesting itself in a premature attempt at social reform. We must proceed to account for its disappearance.

It broke down even in the case of the small society of the "Poor Saints" in Jerusalem. And why? Because an equal share of all in the enjoyment of property demands an equal amount of common labour and skill in all. As that is not possible, ruin follows when all the available surplus of accumulated capital is consumed "among so many," not to speak of the effect of "idleness, selfishness, and unthrift," the rocks on which any ordinary Communistic society would most probably founder.

As an effort at social organisation during the early period of religious enthusiasm this Communism of the primitive Christians deserves our respect. The principle, however, proved inapplicable to the condition of the Church and the world upon further trial. As Dean Milman justly remarks, speaking of the Communism of the Essenes as compared with that of the Christians, " Such a system, however favourable to the maintenance of certain usages and opinions within a narrow sphere, would have been fatal to the aggressive and comprehensive spirit of Christianity; the vital and conservative principle of a sect, it was inconsistent with an universal religion; and we cannot but admire the wisdom which avoided a precedent so attractive, as conducing to the immediate prosperity, yet so dangerous to the ultimate progress of the religion[1].' Although the practice of Communism was given up for practical reasons, or died a natural death, there still remains the spiritual, the living principle, which existed in this effete practice of the early Church.

The noble idea underlying that system is the " great secret " of Christ's religion, the unpalatable doctrine of unselfishness and self-sacrifice; or, in our modern phraseology, it is the doctrine of *Altruism* as opposed to *Egoism*; in a higher sense, the principle of Christian Socialism as opposed to un-Christian Individualism—not the Socialism of the Socialists, but the social theory formulated by St. Paul in his Epistle to the Philippians: " *Look not every man on his own*

[1] " History of Christianity," vol. i. p. 357. On the other hand, see " Conybeare and Howson's Life and Epistles of St. Paul," vol. i. p. 80, where the authors remark : " The Apostolic Church was in this respect in a healthier condition than the Church of modern days."

things, but every man also on the things of others.
Let this mind be in you, which was also in
Christ Jesus." The principle still remains in
force, that all our possessions, as well as all our
gifts, are to be held in trust for the general
good of all—a principle essentially and dis-
tinctively Christian.

This spirit of brotherly love is being more
and more understood in the present day. The
great Communistic principle, " All for each and
each for all," is practically gaining ground. It
is being applied in the case of all our philanthropic institutions; of our hospitals and benevolent societies; our voluntary schools and pious
foundations; our free libraries and museums;
our drinking-fountains and public parks. Its
spirit pervades our mild poor laws—mild to a
fault; our laws for the protection of labour, and
for the provision of healthy homes for the industrial classes, our sanitary reforms, our private
charities and systematic organisation, and the
numberless attempts to alleviate the misfortunes
of the maimed, the halt, and the blind, the
wretched and the fallen; in fact, all efforts of
the State and private individuals and associations to improve the condition of the less privileged members of society. These interferences
of government form practically a voluntary
Communism, being an application of the funds

of the wealthy for the benefit of the poor, a sort of sharing, so to speak, the " wealth of nations " among all, on the pattern of the early Christian Church.

Much has been accomplished in this way; and more yet remains; but whatever is to be done must be done gradually. For the work of God in the world, the progress of Christianity in the heart, the improvement of social relations between man and man—all this is a work of slow growth. It is to be accomplished by a course of gradual development, of steady progress, not by sudden revolutionary changes.

The edifice of society, constructed on this new foundation—the Christian basis—must of necessity be a long time in building. But the completion of the whole plan cannot be helped, though for a time it may be hindered, by the destructive propensities of Communistic agitators on the one hand, and the obstructive measures of the advocates of stationary inaction on the other. The resultant, however, of the two antagonistic forces, both of them coeval with society itself, must be in the future as it has been in the past—Social Progress.

CHAPTER II.

COMMON LIFE IN THE MIDDLE AGES.

IN the last chapter we have spoken of the early favour shown by the Christian Religion to a system of social equality and a community of goods; and we have explained it as being the result of the first outburst of religious enthusiasm. We shall now proceed to show how with every new revival of religious feeling, similar tendencies prevailed, and similar attempts were made to reintroduce communistic institutions, because they were supposed to be in keeping with the spirit of primitive Christianity.

During the first four centuries the fathers of the Church often looked back regretfully to the Apostolic age, when the brethren " had all things in common." Thus, St. Chrysostom exclaims, with a sigh, " If we ourselves adopted in our own day this mode of life, the result would be an immense addition of happiness to rich and poor alike ; both would have an equal share of advantage." St. Basil, and Gregory of Nyssa, give expression to similar sentiments, whilst St. Ambrose uttered those memorable words, which have been re-echoed so often since by social enthusiasts : " Nature has given all things in common to all men. Nature has established a common right, and it is usurpation which has produced a private claim."

Along with these utterances in favour of the simplicity of the early days of Christianity, we find among the writings of the fathers others equally strong in support of the rights of property. In none of them is there any encouragement of schemes for a violent reconstruction of society on purely communistic principles, such as are put forward by modern Socialists.

Many heretical sects also existed during the early years of the Church who, under the pretext of reforming the common faith, would have established Communism as the true basis of Christian social life. Such were the Nicolaitans, the Carpocratians, and the Pelagians, who all looked back to the Communism of the early Christians as the golden age of the Church.

The most decided tendency in this direction, however, manifests itself in the communistic establishments of the monastic orders, and among the so-called heretics of the mediæval revival which preceded the Reformation.

Thus, within the pale of the Romish Church existed the monks and religious orders, and, partly within and partly without, those imitators of apostolic simplicity—the Beghards, Fraticelli, the Cathari, and Brothers of the Common Lot, who all more or less practised Communism on religious grounds, and as a protest against the abuses of private property, which they denominated " that accursed vice of property [1]."

---

[1] Although many of the mediæval sects violently attacked the asceticism of the monastic orders, they were themselves actuated by a similar spirit. In fact this spirit of asceticism was the guiding principle of all the semi-communistic and semi-religious societies which we shall describe further on in this work. Asceticism had its original home among Oriental peoples, who universally believed in the omnipotence of the Absolute or All, and the insignificance and injuriousness of Individuality as involving a separation from the Absolute. This feeling, which was brought to a head in the severe Puritanism of Buddhism, widely affected Eastern nations prior to Christianity. Its influence on the Jews we saw in considering the social system of the Essenes. Among the Greeks it had not much effect, if we except the Pythagorean fraternity. It soon began to make itself felt on the early Christian Church, especially its Eastern branch. When carried to excess, and when its exercise became overloaded with corruption, it led to the violent opposition of the reformers of the Reformation and pre-Reformation period. Yet the same spirit shows itself among the Moravians, the Shakers, and the various communities of the present age, who oppose themselves to the existing order of society.

It would be out of place to give here a full and exhaustive account of all these sects. We must content ourselves with a rapid sketch of the religious communities of the monks during the middle ages, and of the religious brotherhoods towards their close. Noting the state of society in which they arose, we shall show what influence they exercised at the time, for good and for evil, and shall draw attention to the economic, or rather anti-economic, principles which prevent them from serving as models for communistic societies in the present day.

Both in the East and West, among the followers of Buddha and Pythagoras, as well as among the disciples of Christ, there have been men at all times who, either influenced by religious ardour or love of contemplative ease, have sought refuge in retreats, and secluded hermitages, away from the " haunts of men and the vices of society." We have descriptions of early monastic establishments in Egypt attached to the Christian faith. The brothers are described as dressed each in a long linen tunic, bound by a woollen girdle, having over it a cloak, which in its turn was covered by a sheepskin. Sometimes they went about barefoot, and sometimes wore a kind of sandal. Their food was bread and water, their only luxuries were oil and salt, olives and figs, and these were indulged in but rarely and sparingly. They ate in perfect silence, each troup by itself. Every monk had his separate cell, the furniture of which consisted of a mat of palm-leaves and a bundle of papyrus, which served as a pillow by night and a seat by day. They spent night and day in religious orisons, or listened in silence to the reading of the Word. Men of rank and education left their luxurious palaces for these simple abodes in the howling wilderness; they voluntarily deserted their estates and worldly prospects to seek peace for their souls, and immunity from temptation, in monastic seclusion. Like the first Christians of Jerusalem, they held their temporal possessions in common, established regular communities of the same sex, and assumed the names of Hermits, Monks, or Anchorets, expressive of their lonely retreat in a natural or artificial desert [1].

When the Roman Republic was crumbling to pieces from private vices and public corruption, the " Christian Republic " recently founded in its midst preserved it from immediate ruin. So, also, when Roman society, by its selfishness and extravagant luxury, hastened on its own dissolution, the " Republics of Monachism " introduced the counteracting principles of fru-

---

[1] Milman, " History of Christianity," vol. iii. pp. 208-210. Gibbon, " Decline and Fall," chap. xxvii.

gality and self-denial, and so laid the foundations of a reformed society in the midst of social disorganisation.

At a later period, when the incursions of the barbarians laid waste the fertile lands of sunny Italy, in the midst of the desolation and destruction which ensued the monasteries became the shelter of the weak, and their inmates the civilisers of these wild children of the forests.

Thus was formed the nucleus of a new European society. The religious brotherhoods and their disciples became the pioneers of Christianity and of civilisation in unknown wilds, and in lands rendered desolate by the fire and sword of ruthless invaders. The monastic principle of administration upheld the rights of all in an age when rights were almost universally disregarded. Surrounded by "ruined cities, stopped watercourses, cultivated land falling back into marsh and desert—a soil too often saturated with human corpses [1]," the monks reared their common habitations, and did everything in their power to reorganise society. They became the teachers of a new "social science," in accordance with the principles of Divine justice, when all around was injustice and selfish spoliation of the weak by the strong. The

[1] Charles Kingsley, "The Roman and the Teuton," p. 156.

monasteries were the refuges whither "flocked
the poor, the crippled, the orphan, and the widow
— all, in fact, who could not fight for themselves"[1] — and thus maintained, in an age of
remorseless violence, the Christian principle of
compassion.

These Christian settlements, abbeys, or monasteries, were so many industrial centres, in
which every man endeavoured to contribute his
share for the common welfare. They did what
Fourier and Louis Blanc would have made part of
their own systems—they threw their talents and
powers into the common stock. They engaged
in farming, gardening, carpentering, even writing, doctoring, teaching in the schools, or
preaching to the heathen around them on the
associatory principle[2]. Whilst the outer world
presented a ghastly spectacle of violence, fraud,
injustice, cruelty, lustful ambition, and a merci-
less subjection of the weak by the strong, the
monks presented to the world the spectacle of
a society united by a common bond of union
sharing equal rights and duties, where the

[1] Charles Kingsley, "The Roman and the Teuton,"
p. 213.

[2] Ibid., p. 233. Those who wish to obtain a tolerably correct
view of the age and the social influences of Monachism at
the time should read the volume alluded to, especially pp.
154-244, and compare Guizot's "History of Civilisation in
Europe," 4th and 6th Lessons.

strong came to the succour of the weak, and kind forbearance and tender charity formed the rule of daily life.

During the period of Feudalism which followed, when liberty became almost extinct, and every baron became absolute within his own domain ; when a warlike spirit untouched by the softer emotions of pity and brotherly love prevailed ; when the government of Europe fell into the hands of local tyrants, whose oppressive rule "straightened the yoke of the serfs, constrained the free intercourse of the people, perpetuated their ignorance and dependence, and checked their social improvement," the monastery, with its republican government and constitutional laws, served as a model for a reformed society. The monasteries extended their beneficent rule to the municipalities that were slowly gathering around them, and these presently grew into cities which were destined to break the yoke of feudal bondage. "Men talk of democracy," says Charles Kingsley, "those old monasteries were the most democratic institutions the world had ever till then seen [1]."

Thus the moral government of ecclesiastical communities seemed the triumph of law and order over the violence of the feudal lords ; and

---

[1] "The Roman and the Teuton."

when the World in its "pilgrim's progress" had reached the slough of despond in the tenth century, and became subject to absolute and unmitigated despotism, the Church of the day encouraged popular association for the vindication of the common rights, and could point to the monasteries as an example of strength acquired by means of corporate union.

The rise of the middle-class, and of commercial enterprise, was the result, and the establishment of corporate rights and liberties quickly followed. Thus the principles of association, co-operation, and a fair division of labour and enjoyment, fraternal love, and devotion to the common good, lawful obedience under free institutions, and a spirit of beneficence towards those without — in fact the leading principles of all Utopias — found some realisation in these monastic institutions before the dawn of modern civilisation. Monachism gave "a wholesome stimulus to the enervated race" of Romans; it presented a spectacle of social cohesion in a disorganised state of society during the dark ages, and in making manual labour, hitherto despised, the basis of European life, it promoted the rise of the artisan and middle-class, and the triumph of civic liberty over feudal oppression.

What was the cause of such success in these

monastic establishments? Was it Communism
pure and simple as they practised it? We
answer, No! For without the acts of heroism
and self-denial of these religious Communists;
without the rule of celibacy, which prevented an
undue increase of numbers; without the existence of a larger outer world, which to a certain
extent ministered to the wants of these recluses,
their societies, admirably organised and governed as they were, could not have stood the
test of time. They succeeded as "extra-social"
communities altogether separated from the world.
Their constitution, therefore, cannot serve as a
pattern to the world at large, which is not
ready for the austerities of the cloister, or abstinence from the material enjoyments of life,
which formed the leading principles of Monachism. The later history of these societies,
therefore, holds out no encouragement to modern
Communists, who nevertheless point to their constitution as a pattern to modern society. When
no longer satisfied with the monotony of their
daily round of duties, they yielded to the enticing
temptations of dull idleness; when the monks,
who had begun as beggars, became by the
votive offerings of their ignorant admirers as
wealthy as princes, the rules of abstinence and
frugal simplicity were broken or disregarded,
opulence led to corruption, fanaticism under-

mined the principle of brotherly love, and the monasteries themselves became the scenes of rapacity and lust; the sanctities of a common brotherhood being polluted by the wicked conduct of many of its members.

The salt had lost its savour, the Church became secularised, the pious fervour of the monks no longer sustained them in their war against the sensuous brutality of the age—they became themselves the victims of the social exigencies of the times. The ages of asceticism and wholesome restraint (which our modern Communists do not wish to see revived) were followed by a dark period of ecclesiastical corruption, and in vain noble spirits like St. Francis and St. Dominic strove to regenerate the Church and Society by unfurling the " Magna Charta of evangelical poverty."

The depravity of the Church, and the luxury of the hierarchy, led to an "inundation of heresy," and gave birth to a number of sects, who agitated for a return to the simple life of the Apostolic age. At the same time, attempts were made to break through the hard crust of feudalism by several popular movements among the grovelling multitudes of serfs and the rebellious burghers of free cities, who made the eleventh century "a century of insurrection." There was mutiny in the very camp of the

D

Papacy. The *Fratricelli* as a separatist branch of the Franciscan Order in Italy and Spain; the "Brothers of the Free Spirit," a body accused of Pantheistic and Communistic tendencies in Germany and Flanders; the Beghards and Beguinæ, who led a common life, and practised charity among the people around them, all protested against the accumulation of wealth in the Church, and warred against the possession of private property. They began by being social and ended in being religious dissenters. Some, as for example the Beguins, were "tolerated, though, indeed, never actually countenanced, by Rome."

These "paltry brotherlets" were more or less related to the *Cathari*, the Puritans of the middle ages, among whom the "perfect" renounced all personal property, professed to imitate the Saviour and His Apostles in poverty, and declaimed against the wealth and secularity of the clergy[1]. Some among them, like the early Christians, had all things in common[2].

They had numerous followers among the laity. The tesserantes or weavers of the South of France, and the "poor men of Lyons," joined the "poor of the Lord" in their complaints against the wanton despotism of the feudal

---

[1] Robertson, "History of Christian Church," vol. v. p. 324.

[2] Milman, "Latin Christianity," vol. v. p. 402. Third Edition.

lords and the degeneracy of the Church. The
secret working of discontent in the depths of
society made itself felt, and threatened a violent
disruption in the Church and in the world.
A powerful fraternising spirit united the religious sectaries, who formed a sort of *international society* of devout purists in the principal
countries of Europe, and preached the doctrines
of Christian Socialism, whilst they practised
Communism in its various forms. Interdicts,
curses, and active persecution were used to stamp
out spiritual and social heresies. But persecution
only served to extend the doctrines that were
denounced, and to enlist the sympathy of the
populace in favour of the dissentients. It thus
led to the spread of heresy in different directions,
and served to precipitate a series of social insurrections from the twelfth century to the
Reformation.

Among the numerous sects of that day those
which stand out most prominently above the
rest are the Brothers of the Common Lot, or
the Brothers of the Common Life, as they were
called in Germany and the Low Countries, and
the Apostolici who flourished in Italy under
Sagarelli and Fra Dolcino. To their history
and communistic institutions we shall now
direct the reader's attention.

" Dear master," said the younger Florentius

vicar of Deventer, one day to Gerhard the revered preceptor of Thomas à Kempis, "what harm would it do were I and these clerks, who are here copying, to put our weekly earnings into a *common fund* and live together?"

"Well, then," says the master, after a short parley, during which he pointed out the difficulty of the undertaking to his ardent disciple, "in God's name, commence, I will be your advocate, and fully defend you against all who rise up against you." Thus was formed the Society of the Common Lot, which presently grew into an extensive confederation—an *union of brethren* on the Apostolic pattern. The object of its members was by this establishment to extend the usefulness of practical Christianity by the simplicity of their common life, by their rigorous code of morality, and by the introduction of a higher spiritual tone of devotion.

They sought to obtain their object by the propagation of religious knowledge in their schools, and the dissemination of sacred literature copied by the brethren. To provide for their common subsistence without disturbing a purely brotherly relationship among themselves [1], they introduced the principle of *a community of goods*. "Modest subordination," says Thomas

[1] Ullman, "Reformers before the Reformation," vol. ii. p. 71, *et seq.*

à Kempis, "passed among the brethren, from
the highest to the lowest, for the first of virtues,
and made their earthly house a paradise." The
rectors were regarded as the fathers of the
institution, the members were their obedient
sons. Their mode of life was as follows:—
About twenty of them lived together in the
possession of a common fund, and taking their
food at a common table. Some were priests,
some clerics, some laymen. Reception into
the society was rendered difficult, and novices
underwent a rigorous season of probation. The
candidate admitted had to resign his patrimony
for the common use. The customary dress was
of a sombre colour, and a cowl covered the ton-
sured head of the brethren as with monks, although more freedom of attire was allowed than
is usual in the monasteries. The division of time
for labour and devotional exercises was most me-
thodical. Some were engaged in literary labours,
others in manual work, but an interchange of
duties frequently took place so as to secure
variety and cordial co-operation, as was suggested centuries later by Fourier. The government of the whole was partly hierarchical and
partly technical, as was afterwards recommended
by Campanella in his "City of the Sun [1]."

[1] Campanella, a Dominican monk celebrated for his in-
novations in philosophy, was born in 1568 in Calabria. His

Female societies were formed in imitation of these confraternities. A community of women engaged in manual labour was established. They were employed in sewing and weaving, in devotional exercises, and in the instruction of female children, by which means they became instrumental in spreading the principles of the society among families generally.

These institutions, notwithstanding numerous obstacles, spread rapidly, and increased in importance and prosperity, enjoying much popular favour. When they had fulfilled their mission they passed away without a struggle. During the period preceding the Reformation they supplied many pressing needs. They served as an educational agency before the revival of learning, as a co-operative society for transcribing books before the discovery of the art of printing, as a social community "resting on the foundation of apostolical antiquity" at a time when social relations had become strained and social morality had sunk to its lowest ebb —in fact they stood out against the back-ground

interference in politics led to his imprisonment in a Neapolitan dungeon for twenty-seven years. Pope Urban VIII procured his release, and aided in his escape to France, where he was well received by Cardinal Richelieu. An account of his Utopia, called the "City of the Sun," is given in the author's work, "Utopias, or Schemes of Social Improvement," chap. ii. pp. 14-31.

of a dark age like " a peak gilded with the first morning rays in the dawn which precedes the Reformation."

When that great event came, these societies quickly passed away to make room for others more suited to the times. Their success, as far as it went, proves the possibility of active co-operation on communistic principles, if accompanied by the affectionate association of mind and heart, actuated by the highest motives of morality, the spirit of pietism and self-surrender. The application of such principles to the Utopian schemes of most modern Communists, who make material enjoyment and self-indulgence, irrespective of moral considerations, the *summum bonum* of existence, is, therefore, out of the question. As an encouragement, however, to co-operative association, resting on an ethical basis, these social experiments of a past age are of great importance. They teach us that the development and success of co-operative association depend on the growth of a higher motive power manifesting itself in acts of self-denial and brotherly love among all classes of society.

From the flat lowlands of the north we turn to the sunny south, to follow a similar social experiment beyond the Alps among the Piedmontese mountains.

The Apostolicals of Italy, headed by Saga-

relli and Fra Dolcino, differed as much from
the Brethren of the Common Lot as the fiery
temperament of southern nations does from the
cold reserve and calm self-control of the north.

On the Podesda's seat in the market-place of
Parma sits a comparatively young man, dressed
in a white flowing robe, with long white hair
covering his neck and shoulders, and a thick
beard falling over his chest. Round his waist
he wears the cord of the Franciscan friars, but
he does not belong to that order. He has just
sold his small property. He flings the pur-
chase-money, contained in a small leathern
purse, down from the place where he sits among
a crowd of scrambling boys, to show his contempt for the sordid dross, and to begin his
career as a strict follower of the Apostles. This
man is Gerard Sagarelli, "the patriarch and
protomartyr" of Lombard Puritans, the founder
of a new mendicant brotherhood who call themselves the Apostles. Loud and shrill is his
preaching in the streets of Parma. At first
he is despised or pitied by the lookers-on,
but his earnest appeals and hysterical exhorta-
tions soon produce an effect upon the populace.
He becomes the head of an undisciplined though
organised sect—an union of brethren, not held
together by any vow, rule, or law, but actuated
solely by the free spirit of love and a total

renunciation of earthly interests. For nearly twenty years the society is allowed to spread without being molested. At length the spirit of persecution is aroused. Sagarelli, after a short respite of confinement, when every attempt to turn him aside from his heretical opinions fails, although by some he is supposed to have abjured his errors, falls a victim to the Dominican inquisition, and his followers are crushed. A successor of greater intellectual capacity and of stronger will is found in Fra Dolcino of Novara, who becomes the leader of a larger and more formidable society of religious Communists, a society whose history has been considered the most striking episode in the long and sad chronicle of mediæval heresy. A cloud of obscurity and mystery hangs over the earlier life of Fra Dolcino. He is said to have sprung from a noble family, and to have distinguished himself in his studies by quickness of parts and diligence. Before his assumption of the leadership of the sect, on the death of Sagarelli, we find him active as an anti-sacerdotalist in the districts of the Tyrol, denouncing the luxury of the clergy, and recommending a community of goods. His powerful eloquence made a deep impression on his followers, who clung to him with a stern, enduring fanaticism. His tact in organisation and military skill enabled him to hold out for a considerable time against his powerful enemies, who persecuted him as they had his predecessor. We are not here concerned with his religious tenets and apocalyptic predictions concerning the golden age of true Apostolic perfection, which he declared had been lately inaugurated by his predecessor Sagarelli. We must confine ourselves to his social views, and the manner in which he tried to give them effect.

His object was to restore a primitive simplicity of life, and hence he instituted Communism among his followers. But this Communism was nothing else than a universal renunciation of property, a strict equality of distribution. Utter expropriation and self-extinction was the guiding principle of the Dolcinists. Many persons of quality left their estates and joined the society, as well as many of the common people. The peasantry, goaded to madness by feudal exaction, swelled its ranks. Oppressed vassals, citizens of the towns, all priests and friars in rebellion against Rome, "took refuge from want, degradation, and tyranny," in a society which made it its boastful claim to have separated from a " Church, carnal, overburdened with possessions, overflowing with wealth, polluted with wickedness," —a society which proposed to establish a Church

" spiritual, frugal, without uncleanness, admirable for its virtue, with poverty for its raiment [1]."

Their enemies accused them of heinous tenets and hideous morals, charges which, however, deserve but slight credit [2]. One thing is certain, that from the highest motives they discarded the sweets of life, and chose privation, hardship and suffering. Through starvation and misery, against ruthless enemies, under the dire inclemencies of nature, they had to fight their way to the crown of martyrdom.

They shared the common fate of heretics, they were hunted to death. An internecine war, carried on with all the savage cruelty of the time, was waged between Dolcino and his Papal opponents. It ended in his utter defeat, after he had held out with remarkable fortitude on the bleak and inhospitable crags of Monte Calvo and Mount Zerbal. The sufferings and privations of Dolcino and his followers among these inaccessible rocks, covered with ice and snow, called forth the admiring sympathy of Dante, who has commemorated him in these lines—

> " This warning thou
> Bear to Dulcino: bid him, if he wish not

[1] Milman, " Latin Christianity," vol. vii. pp. 371–381, *et passim*.

[2] Cf. L. Mariotti, " Memoir of Fra Dolcino and his Times," p. 208, who defends them against the charges of immoral tendencies and promiscuous marriages.

Here soon to follow me, that with good store
Of food he arm him, lest imprisoning snows
Yield him a victim to Novara's power;
No easy conquest else."

When famine and the sword had reduced
his band of followers, when the besieged, worn
to skeletons, were groping about for food
among the corpses of their fallen comrades,
Mount Zerbal was stormed, and a thousand of
its defenders were massacred, drowned in their
flight in the rivers, or burned at the stake.
Dolcino was made prisoner. He refused to
recant, and after horrible torments, which were
borne with heroic firmness, his body was committed to the flames.

Dolcino's influence, however, was felt long
afterwards among the Cathari of Italy and the
Waldenses in the Piedmontese valleys, although
the sect of the Apostolicals, for a time at least,
was extinguished in blood.

" In Dolcino," to use the words of Neander,
" we see the climax of that ascetical view of
Christian charity, according to which it should
manifest itself, not in the appropriation of all
earthly means for the advancement of God's
kingdom, but in the renunciation of every
earthly advantage ; not in the conciliation and
subordination of the *inequalities of condition
flowing out of human relations, and necessary to*

the various development of man's nature, but in the total abnegation of those differences. In opposition to the worldliness of the Church, he proposed an entire estrangement from the world by *a fraternal association of love,* in which all should be united together under a voluntary bond, independent of constraint and law, and with the repudiation of all property and all inequalities of condition."

To explain the cause of Dolcino's failure we must recognise the necessity of working through existing forms of social life, not by isolation from them. Monastic communism, even if it could exist without the evils inseparable from it, is opposed to the spirit and teaching of the gospel.

A similar error underlies the proposals of modern Socialists for the immediate reconstruction of society. Modern civilisation will prevent the recurrence of the enormities of a less advanced age. Let us hope that the social miscalculations and economic errors of the past will serve as a warning for the future, and that a millennium of failures from the fourth to the fourteenth century will convey a lesson of patience to would-be revolutionisers, and a lesson of hope to the earnest reformers of society.

CHAPTER III.

PRE-REFORMATION SOCIALISMS.

IT has been well observed that there is not an economic problem which was not discussed in the monasteries, in the schools, and the places of public resort during the middle ages. Absolute equality, the abolition of private property, the reward of labour in proportion to personal requirements rather than special aptitudes, in fact all the burning questions which have been agitated by modern Socialists, occupied the attention of, and gave rise to fruitful controversies among, mediæval Churchmen. The canon law, seeking to protect the "patrimony of the poor," favoured equality and strongly opposed the individual acquisition of wealth and the receipt of usury. On the other hand, Thomas Aquinas urged strong reasons in favour of private property. But the balance of mediæval opinion was in favour of equality. To what extent monastic institutions favoured Communistic ideas we have seen in the previous Chapter. There we also

observed how the Church mitigated the over-
whelming poverty of the people, promoted the
accumulation of capital, contributed towards the
restoration of agriculture, and revived within
itself the remembrance and the use of the great
franchise of popular election; how she waged
warfare against all forms of slavery, and, as a
powerful spiritual corporation, fearlessly opposed
the ruthless despotism of the times [1]. Presently
we saw a sudden change of front on the part
of the ecclesiastics, the growth of wealth and
luxury in the Church, accompanied by egre-
gious crimes and follies, rapacity and vice, all
in glaring contradiction to the precepts of the
gospel and the principles of poverty professed
by the mendicant orders. This change, as we
pointed out, led to the appearance of numerous
sects, all protesting against the wealth and
corruption of the clergy. Social reformers
arose, such as Fra Dolcino. Political agitators appeared, like Arnold of Brescia. These
were all men of virtue, and held stern republican
opinions; they were men in whom, as Dean
Milman says, the monk and the republican had
met, who were at the same time admirers

[1] Sir James Stephen, "Lectures on History of France,"
vol. i. pp. 33–37; and with this compare the testimony of so
impartial a witness as Frederick Harrison, in his two lectures
on "The Meaning of History," pp. 67, 68.

of the old Roman liberty and of the lowly religion of Christ, men who may be called the leaders of the Social Democracy of the dark ages. There were, also, the several spiritual societies who desired to imitate the simplicity of social life that existed among the Apostles, as for example that body of primitive people who dwelt in the Piedmontese valleys, from which probably they received their name—the *Waldenses* [1].

This "race of uncorrupted shepherds" discarded all distinctions of rank and station. They wished to confiscate all endowments and privileges of the clergy. They themselves professed "rigid evangelical poverty, and avoided the pursuits by which wealth might be gained." They resembled the Fratricelli in their levelling doctrines, and Peter Waldo, who by some is supposed to have given the sect its name, divided his fortune among the brethren he gathered round him, and became the leader of the " poor men of Lyons," who corresponded to the followers of St. Francis, known as the " poor men of Lombardy." Thus extremes meet. Both

---

[1] From vaux = valley, they were called Vaudois. Many authorities are of opinion that the name is derived from Peter Waldo, a merchant of Lyons in the twelfth century, who was the leader of a wide-spread struggle against the corruptions of the clergy.

Minorites [1] and Waldenses agreed in one point at least—they were alike averse to the corrupting influences of wealth in Church and State, and took upon themselves vows of poverty. The Waldenses expected the reappearance of the Messiah to establish evangelical equality in a society without priests, without nobles, without rich people. Walter Mapes, an Englishman and a Franciscan monk, gives the following description of them from his own personal observation : " They have no settled place of abode. They go about barefoot, two by two, in woollen garments, possessing nothing, but, like the Apostles, *having all things in common*, following naked Him who had not where to lay His head." No one ever has attempted to call in question the honesty or purity of their character. On the contrary, they are spoken of with respect even by their enemies, and described as quiet, modest, and formal in their manners. They avoided commerce as injurious to uprightness of conduct, and chiefly engaged in manual labour. Their Socialism, which was from the first voluntary, was not revolutionary in its tendency, and in their daily life and conduct they were distinguished " by a sincerity, a piety,

[1] Minorites, a name of the Franciscan order, derived from the later denomination adopted by their founder, *Fratres Minores*.

and a self-devotion that almost purified the age in which they lived[1]."

Although admittedly less obnoxious, on account of their peculiar tenets, to the Church of Rome than other sectaries, they shared their common fate—persecution by fire and sword, continued even down to the seventeenth century, when the horrid cruelties and massacre to which they were exposed called forth the noble remonstrance of Cromwell, and inspired Milton's grand ode,

> "Avenge, O Lord, thy slaughter'd saints, whose bones
> Lie scattered on the Alpine mountains cold."

Some of them found refuge in Bohemia, where we shall find them presently allied to a kindred sect, the Hussites, who, with the Lollards in England, kept up the continuity of efforts towards social reform during the pre-reformation period.

We turn now to the Lollards[2], whose connection with the popular movement of the

---

[1] Hallam's "Middle Ages," vol. iii. p. 384.

[2] The name Lollards is derived by some from a German leader of the sect in Cologne, named Walter Lolhard, who flourished about the year 1315, and had about 24,000 followers; but others derive it from *lallen* or *lollen* = making a doleful sound in singing psalms or hymns in an undertone. The term "to loll about" appears to be derived, in a secondary sense, from Lollards, when this name had become a term of opprobrium.

masses in this country during the fourteenth century is peculiarly interesting.

The way had been paved in England for social changes by grievances that loudly demanded social reforms. With the increased sense of the dignity of labour fostered by the Church, and a gradual recognition of personal rights and civic liberty in the rising towns, a spirit of insubordination against the ruling classes, clerical and lay, who had abused their power, showed itself among the masses, not only in this country, but throughout the continent of Europe.

"Pity us, lady, we cannot live, because of this abbot. His servants plunder us, and slander us injuriously. See! they are making you go out of the way, lest our trouble should be manifest to you." Such was the complaint of the villeins of St. Alban's, who flocked round Queen Eleanor for protection against their ecclesiastical oppressors [1]. The same abbey became the scene of conflicts between monks and serfs, between popular aspirations and priestly chicanery, immediately after the rising of Wat Tyler [2]. It furnishes an example of the numerous revolts against ecclesiastical oppression at that time. "The statutes of labourers,"

[1] C. E. Maurice, "Lives of English Popular Leaders in the Middle Ages," vol. ii. p. 74.

[2] Ibid., p. 187.

bearing the stamp and impress of selfish class
legislation in favour of the rich, explain, on
the other hand, the " common cry of curs "
against the landed proprietors [1]. The picture of
English society in the fourteenth century in
Langland's " Vision of Piers Ploughman," where
he contrasts so vividly the frivolous and unreal
splendours of the rich with the simple virtues of
the poor, indicates the seething discontent of the
masses, among whom the poem enjoyed a wide
circulation. " It was," as Mr. Green justly ob-
serves, " the tyranny of property that then, as
ever, roused the defiance of Socialism. A spirit
fatal to the whole system of the middle ages
breathed in the popular rhyme which condensed
the levelling doctrine of John Ball,

> ' When Adam delved and Eve span,
> Who was then the gentleman ?' " [2]

Out of this state of things arose " the strong
Communistic tendency " of the Lollards, who
resembled in this respect their brethren on the
Continent, against whom a papal bull had been
directed, charging them, among other things,

[1] The Statutes of Labourers, passed in the reign of Edward III
(1351–53), regulated the wages of labour and compelled the
workman to serve any employer who required his services.
He was also forbidden to quit his own parish. Green's
" Short History of the English People," p. 242.

[2] " Short History of English People," p. 243.

with their *life in common*. At first, indeed, they only attacked the wealth and luxury of the Church. In the course of events many—especially the more sanguine among them—were inclined to side with the people, and to take up the cause of the "industrious down-trodden rustic poverty," and hence the rising of Wat Tyler and John Ball has been called the Socialist Revolt of the Lollards. Wyclif himself has not escaped from the charge of preaching Communism. In the great struggle between the rich burghers of the towns and the small tradesmen and craftsmen, in the conflict between the "greater folk" and the "lesser folk," we have an early picture of class difference similar to the conflicts between the "Confederation of Employers" and the "Trades Unions" in our own day. At an earlier period the Frith-guilds of merchants and the craft-guilds of tradesmen offered a noble resistance to episcopal and baronial tyranny, and so became "the nursery cradles of popular liberty." But now, when their own independence had been secured, the descendants of the old associates of guilds became themselves proud and overbearing towards their inferiors, and these *nouveaux riches* became as ambitious and tyrannical as the feudal magnates from whose intolerable yoke they had themselves been emancipated. "In the fourteenth century," says Brentano, "commenced the transformation of the trades into entails of a limited number of families—though this number may have been large; and the narrow-minded spirit of capital, petty rivalries, and hateful egotism began to take the place of the great idea of association and solidarity under which the craft-guilds grew up and flourished." Wyclif loudly asserted the principle of Christian fraternity, the common right of all men against this combination of the chief citizens of towns, who sought to exclude their poorer brethren from an equal share in the common privileges, and jealously guarded the boundary line which separated the plebeian workmen from the patrician tradesmen. As Lord Bacon described the guilds as "fraternities of evil" in his day, so Wyclif at this early period says: "All fraternities and guilds made of men seem openly to run in this course. For they conspire many errors against common charity and *common property* of Christian men. And hereto they conspire to bear up each other in the wrong and oppress other men by their wit and power [1]." It is quite impossible to say how

[1] Arnold's edition of Wyclif's English works, vol. iii. p. 335, *apud* Maurice, *loc. cit.* p. 211, where see instances of insurrections against city oligarchies in Bristol, p. 118, London, p. 89, and other municipal struggles of the kind, *passim.* Dr. Wylie in his "History of Protestantism"

far Wyclif and the Lollards sympathised with the popular movement of the time, and to what extent they were carried along by the stream of discontent against the abuses of wealth and property in town and country. But although it has been asserted by an unsympathetic historian that "their notion of property and Church power was wretched and dangerous [1]," there is no evidence to show that any of their tenets favoured compulsory Communism or encouraged a subversion of society.

John Ball, the "mad priest of Kent," as Froissart calls him, indeed professed to be a disciple of Wyclif, and in his harangues to the people gave vent to unmitigated Socialistic opinions, which resemble in a remarkable degree the later utterances of Morelly. Thus he asserts the "original equality of mankind, and that as long as they were governed by the laws of nature, they kept upon even ground, and maintained this blessed purity. That all those distinctions of dignity and degree are inventions of oppression, tricks to keep people out of their

makes Wyclif say with regard to ecclesiastical property, " Let the Church surrender all her possessions—her broad acres, her palatial buildings, her tithes, her multiform dues, and return to the simplicity of her early days." Vol. i. p. 101.

[1] Collier, "Ecclesiastical History of Great Britain," vol. iii. p. 299.

ease and liberty; and, in effect, nothing else but a conspiracy of the rich against the poor [1]." But here and in his wilder and more violent plans of social reconstruction, Ball had probably no more the sympathy of Wyclif and the upper class of Lollards, than have the violent spirits of the Social Democracy at the present moment of the higher clergy and educated classes in Prussia. These however have of late founded a society of State-Socialists, having for its object the improvement of the labouring classes by constitutional means and the avoidance of Socialistic revolution by social reform. Sympathisers among religious and earnest men with

---

[1] Collier, "Ecclesiastical History of Great Britain," vol. iii. p. 149. "Good people," he says in one of his sermons, " things will never go well in England so long as goods be not in common, and so long as there be villeins and gentlemen. By what are they whom we call lords greater folk than we ? On what ground have they deserved it ? Why do they hold us in servage ? If we all come from the same father and mother, of Adam and Eve, how can they say or prove that they are better than we, if it be not that they make us gain for them by our toil what they spend in their pride ? They are clothed in velvet, and warm in their furs and their ermines, while we are covered with rags. They have wine and spices and fair bread ; and we oatcake and straw, and water to drink. They have leisure and fine houses, we have pain and labour, the rain and the winds and the fields, and yet it is of us and of our toil that these men hold their state."—Green's "Short History," p. 243, and see other extracts of " Ball's Letters " in Maurice, *loc. cit.* p. 157, *seq.*

the struggles of the poor there always have been, and will continue to be as long as there remain social grievances demanding redress, which the selfishness of successful worldlings ignores or condemns. Sympathisers of this kind with the popular cause are always liable to be denounced as Socialists by those who are incapable of understanding their objects or the means they would adopt for bringing them about.

Such men are exposed also to the unfavourable criticism of those fiery spirits who blame them for shrinking from violent changes which would imply a total demolition and reconstruction of the social edifice. Whilst, therefore, acknowledging that some of the more fanatical Lollards, especially at a later period, held " Democratic and Communist opinions," and embraced the levelling doctrines of the peasant insurgents, we are far from being convinced that they were, as a body, theoretical Communists, or sought to establish Communism as a Utopian experiment.

John Ball's agrarian revolt, which in many respects resembles the setting up of the French Commune in Paris, came to a speedy end, but not without effecting an improvement in the condition of the labourers [1]. At the same time

[1] " The rebellion was put down, but the demands of the villeins were silently and effectually accorded ; as they were

the statute *de hæretico comburendo*, and similar measures of forcible repression, led almost to the extinction of the Lollard movement. In 1511 a correspondent of Erasmus informs him that wood was dear in England ; and no wonder, when the heretics—*i. e.*, the Lollards—afforded a daily holocaust. Those who still adhered to the opinions of the Lollards at the time of the Reformation furthered no doubt that great movement, and shared the fate of its early martyrs. They may be regarded not only as the forerunners of religious reform, but also in the light of social pioneers engaged in a difficult and dangerous task during a dark age of persecution, and therefore all the more deserving of the recognition and gratitude of later ages.

What Lollardism and the revolt of the peasantry did for England, the Hussites and the peasant wars under Ziska did for Bohemia. There an attempt was made to establish a social Republic, founded on the high principles of

masters for a week of the position, the dread of another servile war promoted the liberty of the serf; and the close of the fourteenth century sees the small freeholder, and probably the tenant in villeinage, . . . important personages in the social order."—J. E. Thorold Rogers, " History of Agriculture and Prices in England," vol. i. p. 8. From this it would appear that Utopian experiments, however futile in themselves, still have indirect effects on the welfare of the people which ought not to be overlooked.

Christian perfectibility; the Church was to be reformed, and all feudal tenures and exclusive privileges were to be abolished. " Good Queen Anne," the wife of Richard II of England, was sister to Wenzel, king of Bohemia, which occasioned at this period a close connection between the two countries. The queen favoured the doctrines of Wyclif, and Jerome of Prague taught in the Bohemian University the doctrines propounded by the cultured Lollards in Oxford. Even the pantomime of leading the insurgents, performed in London by Richard II, was faithfully copied by the Bohemian king in his feigned patronage of the popular rising. The Socialist revolt in both countries was brought to a close amidst fire and bloodshed. Fearful excesses were perpetrated on both sides, and the aspirations of the people were suppressed for a time by force and cajolery, but only to be revived with redoubled force when a second Socialistic wave passed over Europe in the storm-tossed days of Luther's Reformation. But there was this difference, in England the movement produced a race of martyrs, in Bohemia it converted a nation into heroes.

The burning of John Huss at the Council of Constance provoked throughout Bohemia a storm of indignation against the persecutors. The king, the nobles, and the people denounced the treachery of Sigismund and the barbarous injustice of the Council. Ziska showed the feeling of the people. But in his case personal hatred of the priests and national antipathy added force to his determination to break the unbearable yoke of sacerdotal tyranny and foreign thraldom. He is described as traversing with pensive brow and folded arms the long corridors of the palace, which looks down on the broad stream of the Moldau, on the towers of Prague, and on the plains beyond, which stretch towards that quarter of the horizon where the pile had been kindled for the burning of Huss. King Wenzeslaus, surprised by his moody appearance, inquires, " What is this?" His chamberlain replies, " I cannot brook the insult offered to Bohemia at Constance by the murder of Huss[1]." There and then Ziska extorts from the king a permission, granted with incredulous reluctance, to take measures of revenge. Armed with this royal patent, Ziska and the burghers of Prague rose in insurrection immediately upon the publication of a papal bull, authorising a crusade against the Hussites. This was the beginning of the Hussite wars, which lasted for sixteen years— " years of terrible and fatal glory in the history of Bohemia, of achievements marvellous as to valour, military skill, patriotism, and the passion

[1] Wylie, " History of Protestantism," vol. i. p. 183.

for civil and religious freedom[1]." With these wars, " the thundering roll of Ziska's chariots, the shrieks of cities stormed, the wails of armies mowed down by the scythe," we are not here concerned. We are rather attracted by a simple and affecting scene on Mount Tabor in Bohemia, where 42,000 persons of the Hussite community partake of the Holy Communion, followed by a love-feast, at which the rich share their property with their poorer brethren. Out of this celebration grew a society of Christian Communists known as the Taborites, who built a town named Tabor, and spread their political creed and social ideas throughout the kingdom. Thus a new Christian republic on the principle of a community of goods was established, the second advent of Christ was expected, and along with it a final restitution of all things. Multitudes hastened to lay their property at the feet of the clergy, as in the days of the Apostles; and a state of society free from pain and bodily necessities was looked forward to as on the eve of appearing.

This was the creed of the more radical and democratic party. They called each other brothers and sisters; they divided equally among themselves their substance, after the pattern of the early Christians; their manner

[1] Milman, " Latin Christianity," vol. viii. p. 337.

of_ life was grave, and similar to that of the more rigid Puritans, with whom, indeed, they had much in common. As a practical result of this Utopian experiment, we are informed that there were no contentions, no peculations, and no boisterous festivities. All united in heart and will, like the Apostles of old, and sought nothing else but what would conduce to the salvation of souls and the return of the clerical order to the original state of the Primitive Church[1].

The less advanced party required only a renunciation of goods on the part of the clergy, and insisted chiefly on the administration of the Holy Communion in both elements, and hence were called the Calixtenes (calix = cup). They flourished mainly in Prague, where we find them in communion with a small remnant of Waldensians. Virulent opposition and severe persecutions on the part of their enemies, the Imperialists, led to fierce reprisals on the part of the Hussites, who finally degenerated into a herd of "ferocious and desperate fanatics," destroying in their blind fury stately palaces and lofty cathedrals, ravaging cities, and devastating the country, plundering churches and monasteries, and doing the work of cruel incendiaries. Manufactures and commerce came

[1] Gieseler, "Ecclesiastical History," vol. v. pp. 128–130, note No. 17.

to an end; the manners and habits of the
people became coarse and violent; the Taborite
forces, recruited with foreign adventurers, lost
their religious character. Still going forth with
the chalice on their banner as " God's war-
riors," they would scarcely be distinguished from
their enemies who were engaged in warfare
mainly for the purposes of spoil and rapine. The
movement itself was quelled in blood, and the
eleven splendid victories of Ziska were followed
by defeats, until at last a compromise was
arrived at between the contending parties,
which terminated a destructive civil war without effecting any permanent changes in the
social condition of the people. To judge of the
effect of this Utopian experiment, we must
revisit the " Mount of Transfiguration," as they
termed their own Tabor, about thirty years
after the scene had been enacted there which
has been described on a previous page.

Æneas Sylvius Piccolomini was sent as envoy
to confer with the Bohemians on matters in
dispute between them and the Emperor of
Germany. He visited Tabor, and found the
people rude, though not unwilling to be civilised. Their hospitality was rough, though
hearty; their outward appearance showed signs
of poverty; scanty clothing, and houses built
of wood and clay, and arranged like tents, out

of which the town had grown, betokened a retarded civilisation. The warlike character of the people was still shown by the profusion of spoil, accumulated in marauding expeditions. But as this resource became unremunerative, the Taborites had found it necessary to return to commerce, and to abandon the principle of community of goods.

Such was the unsatisfactory result of an ill-organised society, modelled on the plan of a Communistic Utopia and founded in one of the most turbulent ages of modern history. It was affected, no doubt, in its growth and decay by the unsettled condition of the times, and was exposed, moreover, to the constant opposition of the supreme powers both in Church and State.

Ignorance of economic laws, and a consequent inability of the leaders to organise the new society on a satisfactory basis, prevented the establishment of industrial institutions which would provide a means of livelihood in times of peace. Social competency, not to say social progress, under such circumstances, was out of the question. When the available wealth of the Taborites had been divided equally among all and consumed; when the spoils of war had ceased to replenish the stores of the community, want and necessity made their appearance, followed by the consciousness that a return to the old order had become necessary to preserve the people from starvation.

We have now run through a whole cycle of religious communities, which appeared one after another on the stage of history during a period of several centuries, all endeavouring to re-establish the simple life of the Primitive Christians, and all, in turn, failing in their Utopian experiments, although sustained by the strongest faith and the most marvellous enthusiasm.

If we follow these efforts at social reform from the seventh to the fourteenth century—from the exodus of the Paulicians [1] out of Pontus and Cappadocia, when, driven by persecution westwards, they settled in Bulgaria, Croatia, and Dalmatia, presently to appear in Italy, France, Germany, England, and Hungary, under the various names of Cathari, Apostolicals, Fratricelli, Beguins, Waldenses, Albigenses, Lollards, and Hussites, we shall find a recurrence of the same cycle of ideas exhibited in similar effects and meeting with similar rebuffs on the part

[1] The Paulicians, whose origin is wrapped in some mystery, are supposed to have been affected by Manichæan doctrines, which led to their persecution under the Eastern Empire, especially by the Empress Theodora (841–855 A. D.). This caused their separation, and it is from the Paulician settlers in Bulgaria that Catholic historians consider most of the heretical spirit of the pre-Reformation period to have come. See Mosheim's " Ecclesiastical History," and Gibbon's " Decline and Fall," ch. 54.

F

of the outer world, and finally being dissolved on account of faulty internal organisation. There is the same undying aim to re-establish social life on the pattern of Apostolical simplicity; there is the same blending of secular and sacred duties of humanity; there is the same protest against luxury in the Church, and the same impatient revolt against social inequality in the world, and with them a willingness to suffer martyrdom in the cause, and to undergo self-inflicted privations for the purposes of self-discipline; there is the same desire to be "good with a goodness serviceable to the common cause," a desire which cannot be quenched by persecutions of the most cruel kind, nor damped by the severest disappointments. Nay, what is still more remarkable, notwithstanding the lessons taught by the disastrous consequences of these Utopian experiments, we find the feeble remnant saved from the general destruction banded together once more in the same cause. The *Unitas fratrum*, the Moravian Brethren (to be considered in a later chapter) extricating themselves from the wreck and ruin of the Hussite party, and joined by a few surviving Waldenses, in the face of a bitter opposition, drew together and established a community on what has proved to be an enduring and successful foundation.

The continuity of such an irresistible movement deserves respectful attention, its failures
should convey a wholesome lesson to rash
levellers, its marvellous revivals after repeated
discomfiture ought to arrest the attention of
even the superficial antagonist of all social experiments, whilst its indirect influences must
form an important factor in social development,
and deserve the most profound study of the impartial historian of society.

CHAPTER IV.

BEFORE Luther made his perilous entry into Worms as the champion of the Reformation, his friend, Spalatin, anxious for his safety, reminded him of the fate of his forerunner, Huss. Luther's noble reply was, " Huss was burned, but not the truth with him." This pregnant saying applies both to the religious and social movements, which, crushed for a time, were revived and brought to a culmination in what has been called "the Protestant Revolution." The social experiments fostered by the Primitive Church, by mediæval sectaries and by the precursors of the Reformation, were followed up by those futile attempts at reform in the sixteenth century—the Peasant wars of Germany and the Communistic efforts of the Anabaptists. There is a close, though not an historical, connection between the Hussite wars and these movements; just as the Peasants' War itself formed, according to Louis Blanc, the prologue of the French Revolution. All Utopian movements are only so many successive symptoms of the same social malady, whilst Utopias themselves are the prescriptions, and Utopian experiments the treatment, applied to chronic disease in the social organism.

As the early establishment of Christianity in the Roman empire led to a social regeneration, so the re-establishment of Primitive Christianity in feudal Europe at the time of the Reformation was accompanied by a fresh attempt to free mankind, not only from religious thraldom, but also from social bondage.

It has been pointed out that the Reformation not only caused considerable economic changes of a *material* kind, but also was itself hastened on by "social progress, one aspect of the economic side of which shows itself in the discovery of the New World, and the consequent revolution of prices."

To what extent this affected the position of the English peasantry has been shown by Mr. Seebohm in his remarkable little book on the Reformation [1]. Material improvement and a more extensive distribution of comforts among all classes, and the awakening of a spirit of cupidity and curiosity by these discoveries,

---

[1] " Era of the Protestant Revolution," p. 227.

caused the masses all over Europe to become discontented with their material condition. For it is not in periods of the most abject distress that social dissatisfaction is most deeply felt. It is when pressure is partially removed that the "imperious demand for progress" makes itself heard. It is during the dawn which precedes a new era of freedom that the "insurrection of the human mind" breaks out most violently against the abuses of absolute power in Church and State. That this is usually the case may be seen in the great religious and social convulsions of the sixteenth century.

The first manifestation of this great movement, regarded in its social aspect, was the formation of the "League of Shoes," towards the close of the fifteenth century. Under that name the peasantry living in the boundaries of Switzerland formed themselves into a secret alliance to shake off the yoke of their feudal oppressors. From thence the movement gradually spread towards the north and east of Germany, until it assumed the character of a formidable organisation, which was closely connected with the efforts towards religious reform of the time. Thus the programme of the party demanded "Christian union and fraternity." On the banner of these "shoeless ruffians" were depicted the Virgin Mary and

St. John, the Pope and the Emperor, a peasant kneeling before the cross, a *bundschuh* (*i.e.* a peasant's clog), and under it the motto, " O Lord, help the righteous."

During the discussions at the Diet of Worms, in 1521, threats of a general rise of the peasantry were heard in the streets without, and a placard was found posted on the walls of the town-hall, stating that 400 knights and 8000 foot were ready to defend Luther against the Romanists. It had no signature, but underneath were written the ominous words : " Bundschuh, Bundschuh, Bundschuh." This was supposed to have been posted at the instigation of the potent knight Von Sickingen, the " German Ziska," who, it was hoped at one time, would head the common people in their attempt to liberate themselves from both Romanism and Feudalism.

It is interesting to watch these struggles for social freedom three centuries ago, as almost a perfect parallel between them and the present Socialistic conflict in the same country may be instituted. Indeed the attempt has been made by Engels, the friend of Karl Marx, in a preface to his short history of the Peasants' War. Then, as now, a *Culturkampf*, *i. e.*, a struggle between the ecclesiastical pretensions of Rome and the secular power of German princes, accompanied the Socialistic ferment; then, as now, the democratic section of the industrial towns inclined them to side with the revolutionary party. The gates of Würtzburg were thrown open to the rebel army, and the citizens received them with acclamation. But then, as now, the fear of a needy Proletariat demanding material equality terrorised the *bourgeoisie* into submission, at the sacrifice of constitutional liberties to secure themselves against the turbulent section of social levellers. Then, as now, leaders of undoubted power, moral worth, and exalted station, like the eloquent scholar, Ulrich von Hutten, and the valiant knight, Florian von Geier, headed the movement; but also a mixed multitude of malcontents, whose influence was eminently demoralising, were to be found in the camp of the rebels, and in the communal insurrections of the towns. In fine, then, as now, society was in a confused state of mutual distrust, class antagonism, and seething discontent. Along with the cry for State centralisation in favour of the masses, discord and disunion prevailed among the Socialist party, which made them victims of treacherous demagogues like Goetz von Berlichingen, and brought their plans into confusion, until all ended in utter failure.

Fifty years after the suppression of the

Bohemian revolt described in the last chapter, the murmurs of discontent which had been heard for two centuries throughout Western Europe were re-echoed by the peasantry of Germany. In England, the rising of Wat Tyler; in France, the *Jacquerie*, seconded by the mutinous population of Paris; in the Flemish towns, the democratic movement, led by Philip von Artevelde, had preceded the agrarian revolution of Germany. As distant peals of thunder, attended by the lightning flash, precede a powerful storm, so these repeated popular outbursts, succeeded by the brilliant blaze of the "new learning," ushered in the wild tempest of the Reformation period. Popular aspirations could no longer be repressed, and the expressions of the people's wrongs could no longer be silenced.

> " And, cloud-like in their increase,
> All their grief
> Broke, and began the overwhelming wail
> Out of a common impulse, word for word."

The chief grievances of the German peasantry were heavy feudal burdens and exactions, which, with an unjust expropriation of the small holders of land by the cupidity and legal chicanery of the nobles, caused an universal distress among the people. An agrarian Proletariat was created where the memory of their free ancient Germanic village communities had not yet been entirely extinguished. The insolence of local magnates and rising princes in compelling the peasant and the burgher to minister to their expensive luxury and wasteful prodigality, swelled the torrent of popular indignation[1]. In a similar manner the oppressive conduct of the patrician merchants of the towns roused a spirit of rebellion among the small tradesmen and craftsmen, and so increased the number of malcontents throughout the length and breadth of Germany.

Joss Fritz, a soldier of commanding presence and great natural eloquence, suddenly appeared in the Black Forest in 1512–13, with the intention of organising an insurrection among the peasantry; but the conspiracy was betrayed before the contemplated rising could take place. Nevertheless, the rebellion spread secretly, and found numerous adherents in Swabia and Franconia. Soon the charming environs of the Neckar and the Rhine, now so much frequented by tourists, became the scenes of cruel war and

---

[1] Menzel, in his history of the Germans, gives a case illustrating the overbearing insolence of the landed aristocracy of the period. In several places the peasants were compelled to beat the water of the moats during the night so as to keep the frogs from croaking, lest the spiritual or temporal lords inhabiting the castles should be disturbed in their sleep by the noise.

savage devastation in the conflict which ensued between the serfs and their masters.

The demands of the peasantry were comprehended in twelve articles, which, apart from the vague impracticability of some among them, were extremely moderate. They were as follows :—

1. That they should have the right to choose their own pastors.

2. That they should pay tithes of corn, for the support of the pastor and for the use of the parish, but they refused to pay small t'thes.

3. That they should be free, and no longer serfs and bondmen.

4. That wild game and fish should be free to all.

5. That the woods and forests should belong to all for fuel.

6. That no services of labour should be greater than those required of their forefathers.

7. That if more were required wages should be paid accordingly.

8. That rent, when above the value of the land, should be properly valued and lowered.

9. That the punishments for crimes should be fixed.

10. That common land should be again given up for common use.

11. That death gifts (*i. e.*, the right of the lord to take the best chattel of the deceased tenant) should be abolished.

12. That any of these articles proved to be contrary to the Scriptures or God's justice should be null and void.

These reforms were refused, and an army was sent in the year 1525 to reduce the Swabian peasants to obedience, under the command of Truchsess, who crushed the revolt with his trained soldiers in several battles along the Danube, the Algau, and the Bodensee, inflicting heavy losses on the vanquished. Six thousand peasants then assembled in the valley of the Neckar to avenge the slaughter of their brethren in the south. The first victim of their wrath was the young Count of Helfenstein, who lived at the castle in the town of Weinsberg, and who had, by his overbearing cruelty, provoked the deadly hatred of the peasants. They stormed the town and castle, under the leadership of Florian Geier, Wendel Hipler, and Little Jack Rohrbach. The count's offer of ransom was refused. "He must die, though he were made of gold," was the relentless reply of the exasperated peasants. Hipler counselled moderation at a council held after plundering the castle and monastery. But Little Jack held another council of his own in the depth of night, and there every knight and noble in Weinsberg was doomed to death. As day was breaking the count and other noble prisoners were led forth, surrounded by a circle of pikes with the steel points inward. The tears and pleadings of the countess, with a babe in her arms, availed nothing. The peasants stood in two parallel lines, with a passage between the points of their pikes. A piper of the count mockingly led the way, inviting his late master to follow in a dance of death. The count and nobles were compelled to march through. The ranks closed upon them, and they were soon pierced to death. A wild peasant woman stuck her knife into the count's body, and smeared herself with the blood. And thus, unknown to the other leaders, and to the remainder of the peasantry, "Little Jack," on that terrible morning, revenged the thousands of his comrades slain by the Swabian lords, and had blood for blood [1].

[1] Seebohm, "Era of the Protestant Revolution," pp. 139, 140. "A yell of horror," adds the historian, "was raised through Germany at the news of the peasants' revenge. No yell had risen when the count cut the peasants' throats, or the Swabian lords slew thousands of peasant rebels. Europe had not yet learned to mete out the same measure of justice to noble and to common blood."

Other enormities followed : abbeys were sacked ; castles were razed to the ground ; cities were pillaged by the infuriated populace. They plundered the granaries, emptied the cellars, drew the seigneurial fish - ponds, and burnt the convents, all in revenge for wrongs suffered through centuries of oppression. Acts of retaliation, however, followed, in which the savagery of the nobles surpassed even the cruelty of the rebels. Bands of peasants were hewn down by disciplined troops under Truchsess. One night, after a bloody battle, in which several thousand peasants were slain, the piper of Weinsberg, taken among the prisoners— the same who had piped the dance of death at the murder of the Count of Helfenstein— met his fate. In the presence of the survivors, and by orders of the commander, he was fastened with an iron chain, about two feet long, to an apple-tree. With their own hands the nobles helped to build a circular pile of wood round the victim, which they then set on fire. In the depth of night, and amid the groans of the peasants wounded and dying on the battle-field around them, and the drunken revelry of the camp, might be heard the laughter of these nobles as they watched their victim spring shrieking from point to point of the fiery circle, within which he was slowly being roasted to death.   Such was the revenge of the nobles upon the peasantry.

Still the movement spread.   Spires, the Palatinate, Alsace, and Hesse, accepted the twelve articles.   From Lorraine to the Austrian Alps, from the Lake of Constance to the confines of Westphalia, the Peasants' War filled men's hearts with fear, and Hutten's prophecy seemed on the eve of fulfilment: "Should it come some day to an insurrection of the people, it will not be a question how much this person or that person has contributed in bringing about this catastrophe, and who deserves the vengeance of the people.   The innocent and guilty alike will have to suffer in the midst of blind violence and confusion."

It is unnecessary to follow the whole course of this unfortunate outburst of popular indignation.   It would be harassing to describe the bloody scenes which were enacted, and the heartless reprisals of which both sides were guilty.   Suffice it to say that 100,000 peasants lost their lives in the rebellion, or twenty times as many human beings as fell during the Reign of Terror in the French Revolution.

There were two tendencies at work during this great rebellion.   There were the efforts of the peasants simply to shake off ecclesiastical and feudal tyranny, and there were the efforts of the religious enthusiasts to bring about a realisation of the Millennial era and the total regeneration of society on the principle of primitive equality.

It is true the peasants did not always keep to their moderate programme of social reform. One of them said to the Count of Tübingen, "Brother George, thy body is as my body, and my body is as thy body; thy property is my property, and thy property is my property in Christ; we are all brothers and equals." But such cases were exceptions. The battle cry, "Omnia Simul Communia," was not raised among the peasants, but by the Communistic fanatics among the Anabaptists. Müntzer, the chief of this extreme party, demanded the confiscation of all ecclesiastical property to assist in establishing a *universal community of goods*, and he wished the German empire to be, at the same time, transformed into *a Republic, one and undivided;* in fact, he anticipated by three hundred years the demands of Modern Socialism in Germany.

Thomas Müntzer was a minister of Zwickau, and a disciple of Storch, who had been the means of drawing Luther from his retreat at the Wartburg to put down an outbreak of fanaticism at Wittenberg. Müntzer, deposed from his cure, retired to Alstatt, in Thuringia. Here he advanced far beyond the extreme party at Wittenberg, and sought to establish a kingdom of God upon earth with equality and community of goods, intending to compel the ruling princes to submission, according to his own confession[1]. He became the chief agitator of the Peasants' War, and revived in the town of Mühlhausen the social order of the Hussites on Mount Tabor.

His eloquence, inspired by a mystic fanaticism, his prophetic utterances and vehement denunciations of the existing state of things, his strange fantastic mien and evident earnestness, supported by an appeal to dreams and visions, produced a deep impression upon the common crowd, already sufficiently excited by the stirring events of the time. Words like the following fell upon the public ear as sparks into a powder magazine :—

"We have one common father Adam ; whence, then, comes this diversity of ranks and of goods? Why groan we in poverty while others have delicacies ? Have we not a right to the equality of goods which, by their nature, are made to be parted without distinction among us ? Return us the riches of the time being, restore us that which you retain unjustly."

On the other hand, in his religious mysticism and wild denunciations against the corruptions

[1] Gieseler, "Ecclesiastical History," v. p. 344.

of the Christianity of his day, and his high aims at the subjection of the flesh and the regeneration of human nature, he manifests the intense spirituality of Savonarola. The materialistic leanings of Modern Socialism are absent from the teaching of the Anabaptist, although his followers, in establishing a Communistic society in Münster, soon departed from the austere morality and ascetical simplicity of their spiritual ancestor.

"We fleshly human beings," he says, "must become gods by the incarnation of Christ, and by Him must be taught to become etherealised and entirely transformed into His likeness, so that our earthly life may be translated into the heavenly."

As a "prophet of revolution," he stands midway between the ascetic mysticism of the Mediæval Revivalists and the austere sobriety of the Puritans.

Müntzer shared the common fate of Social Revolutionists. He was placed between the horns of a formidable dilemma. He had to choose between putting in practice the extreme and almost impossible schemes of his more advanced followers, or else adopt a course dictated by reason and conscience, but which would be offensive to the surging masses behind him, ever urging him onward. He passed the Rubicon, and decided in favour of extreme measures. He established a community of goods in Mühlhausen, where he exercised, as the apostle of Communism, an unlimited power for nearly a year, and from whence he sent forth the following wild proclamation, hoping by it to extend his kingdom far beyond the city:—

> Arise! fight the battle of the Lord! On! on! on! Now is the time; the wicked tremble when they hear you. Be pitiless! Heed not the groans of the impious! Rouse up the towns and villages; above all, rouse up the miners of the mountains. On! on! on! while the fire is burning! On! while the hot ground is yet reeking with the slaughter! Give the fire no time to go out, the sword no time to cool! Kill all the proud ones: while one of them lives you will not be free from the fear of man! While they reign over you it is no use to talk of God. Amen.
>
> > Given at Mühlhausen, 1525.
> > Thomas Müntzer, servant of
> > God against the wicked.

The storm thus invoked by the deluded visionary overtook him but too soon, and placed him and his poor followers, whom he had organised for defensive warfare, in imminent danger. The Landgraf of Hesse, the Duke of

Brunswick, and the Electors of Mainz and Brandenburg marched their troops against him, and the armies stood facing each other near the town of Frankenhausen. The insurgents were troubled. A proclamation was issued recommending them to surrender, and, on condition of delivering up their leaders, promising a full amnesty. There is hesitation in the camp, and some are ready to capitulate. Müntzer rises and addresses them in words of burning eloquence, which rouse up the old enthusiasm and fill his followers with supernatural confidence. " To-day we shall behold the arm of the Lord," he cries, " and all our enemies shall be destroyed." At this moment a rainbow appears. It is, also, the emblem on the flags over their heads, and they regard it as a rare intimation of Divine favour. Müntzer, remarks the effect and takes advantage of it. " Fear nothing," he exclaims, enthusiastically, " I will catch all the balls in my sleeve." The signal of attack is given in the enemy's camp ; the army is put in motion ; the peasants stand still like a rock. They sing the hymn, " Come, Holy Ghost," and wait for Heaven to declare in their favour. But behold their ramparts are broken down, death rages in the midst of them, dismay takes hold of their ranks, they flee in all directions panic-stricken. Five thousand perished in the general disorder that followed. Müntzer sought refuge in concealment, but was discovered, imprisoned, and finally beheaded [1].

Thus ended the first episode of Anabaptist Communism. Its success was ephemeral and by no means encouraging. Industry was interrupted among the members of the new society. With idleness a rapid dissipation of former savings of course took place, and this was the only result of a temporary Communism under a despotic theocracy. Resting, as it did, on economic fallacies, and subject as it was to political misrule, the ultimate result of this Utopian experiment must have been social disruption and general indigence, even if the society had not been put down by main force.

Another experiment, similar in kind, but, if possible, still more disastrous in its ultimate development, remains yet to be mentioned, the establishment of a Communistic Commonwealth in the city of Münster, the capital of Westphalia, in 1534–35.

A number of Anabaptists, exiled from Switzerland, had settled in Holland, and among them John Matthias of Haarlem, a man of scanty erudition, but gifted with popular elo-

[1] Merle d'Aubigné, "History of the Reformation" (Tract Society's ed., vol. iii. p. 383).

quence, who soon attained great influence and notoriety. One of his disciples was Bernard Rothmann. He belonged to that class of harmless but uneasy spirits who, possessing culture, religious earnestness, and moral worth, but lacking balance of mind, are apt to exercise an unsettling influence on those around them. Rothmann was Protestant pastor of Münster, and, after passing through various phases of religious belief, had embraced with genuine zeal the new doctrine, and now sought with the ardour of a convert and the fervid eloquence of a social innovator to spread his principles in Münster. In this he was vigorously supported by Knipperdolling, a citizen of some position, distinguished for his undaunted courage and thoroughness of purpose, as well as for his turbulent spirit and personal vanity. It is to his baneful influence we are to ascribe many of the subsequent excesses of the Revolutionary party.

By the united efforts of these two energetic agitators an entire revolution in the municipal government of the city was effected, and the principal power was lodged in the hands of Matthias and John of Leyden, who suddenly appeared on the scene to establish the new " Kingdom of Heaven." This victory was not obtained, however, without a struggle with the ruling powers, which was attended with much violence and destruction of property, but ended in the final triumph of the Socialist party. A community of goods was established. All the available property in the city was collected into a common treasury, and under the directions of Matthias, the necessaries of life were distributed to all by the deacons appointed for the purpose, Rothmann being one of them. To spread their tenets beyond the confines of Münster a military expedition was dispatched into Holland and Friesland, with Matthias at the head. He lost his life in the campaign, and was succeeded by his brother in arms, John of Leyden.

This remarkable man was a strange compound of the religious enthusiast and the licentious impostor. Of striking personal appearance and dignified bearing, and undoubtedly gifted with quick intelligence, he knew how to impress the multitude with a deep sense of his own superiority. When left in sole possession of the field, and endowed with supreme power in the newly-founded Commonwealth, he soon became the victim of his own insatiable ambition and inordinate love of sensuous enjoyment. He threw off by degrees his original character of prophet and assumed the prerogatives of royalty, without abdicating altogether his spiritual pretensions. He received the adulation of the people as King of Zion, and his court soon became noted for all the pompous luxuries and effeminate enormities of an Asiatic seraglio; nor were there wanting the proverbial cruelties and petty tyrannies of Eastern despots in this newly-founded " Society of Equals."

Teaching the reconciliation of the flesh and of the spirit, the citizens of Zion indulged in festivities and sensuous delights which strangely contrasted with the earlier austerities of the prophets of equality and the severe teaching of Müntzer.

This state of anarchy was brought to a close by the fall of Münster after a prolonged siege, conducted by the prince-bishop, from whom the city had revolted. For two years John of Leyden had been absolute ruler. He was only twenty-five years old when the city was taken. He was executed after being subjected to cruel tortures, and his body was exposed in a wire cage in the belfry of St. Lambert's Cathedral, where his bleached bones were still exhibited during the last century, a horrible monument of this final episode in the history of Social experiments during the Reformation period.

Thus a movement which, fourteen years before, had begun with comparatively moderate

demands for social reform, ended in a wild Socialistic extravaganza. As the struggle went on, the
rebels had become more and more exasperated
by virulent opposition and defeat, until at last
the " robust vandalism " of the peasants was
succeeded by the mad frenzy of the religious
visionaries, and the dying movement in its final
gasp spent itself in the irrational outbreak of the
Münster Communists.   Thus what had commenced as a protest against the self-indulgence
of the few at the expense of the many ended
in the unbridled self-indulgence of all.   Soon,
however, want of resources, famine and the
sword put an end to this terrible saturnalia of
deranged enthusiasts.   Their blind delusions
and lawless extravagance retarded the progress
of social reform for centuries.   Men, like
Erasmus and More, the author of "Utopia,"
who in their writings had encouraged the
revival of ideals of universal equality, recoiled
with pain and horror from the effects of their
own words, whilst the actual leaders of the
German Reformation, like Luther[1], alarmed
at the consequences of such philosophical
speculations as were displayed in the rising of

[1] His enemies taunted him with the saying, " Luther has
led the people out of Egypt (i.e. Popery) through the Red
Sea (i.e. the bloody Peasant wars), but left them behind in
the wilderness (i.e. the final effort to free themselves from
serfdom)."

Münster, and in the enormities of John of Leyden, used all their influence for the suppression of the movement.

In the short and imperfect sketch we have given of the two great Socialistic movements of the period of the Reformation we may see exemplified the truth of the following verdict of a candid judge on the Socialistic ideal: " Its character as an ideal is highly vague and flexible. It is very largely shaped by the individual minds that hold it. It has a germ in it fruitful of good, and herein lies its power; *but that germ of good has been mixed from the very first with evil elements, which have at times displayed themselves in extraordinary iniquities* [1]." In the next paper on the Social experiments of the Moravian Community we shall have an opportunity of noticing the influences of the same ideal on a state of society slowly and peacefully developing out of similar beginnings, but making Christian self-sacrifice for the common good the rule of life, thus introducing lasting and beneficent social reforms while avoiding Socialistic revolutions.

[1] "Quarterly Review," No. 288, Art. "1877," p. 397.

CHAPTER V.

THE MORAVIAN BROTHERHOOD.

IN the year 1715 an humble petition was presented to the House of Parliament "from
bishops and clergy of the Reformed Episcopal
Churches first settled in Bohemia, and since
forced, by the persecution of their enemies, to
retire into Great Poland and Polish Prussia." An
order of the Privy Council was at the same time
issued "for the relief and for preserving the
Episcopal Churches in Great Poland and Polish
Prussia." But although the Archbishop of Canterbury, the Bishop of London, and other influential friends rendered material help to the
petitioners, the two Acts of Parliament recog-
nising their Church in these isles, and protecting
their missionaries in the colonies, were not
passed till the years 1747 and 1749. About the
same time Count Zinzendorf, the founder of the
modern Moravian brotherhood, was restored to
royal favour in Saxony, and reinstated in his

rights and possessions, after ten years of exile and deprivation. Thus the ancient society of the United Brethren found a refuge in this country in the days of persecution, and what was of still greater importance it was nourished and kept from dissolution by help from private sources. These reasons, as well as the fact that there are still existing settlements of the Moravians in England, ought to render their social schemes especially interesting to the English reader [1].

We cannot here enter into anything like a history of the United Brethren. We must content ourselves with a short account of their social constitution, which demands our notice because its success is being constantly referred to by Socialistic writers as affording encouragement to similar efforts for the reconstruction of society.

In speaking of the United Brethren we must distinguish two branches, so to speak, of the same stem—the Hutterites and the Herrnhuters [2]. The former, or followers of Hutter, after the defeat of the rebel peasants

[1] The members of the Moravian community in this country amount now to 5,645 out of 31,141, which constitutes the whole strength of the society. The chief seat of Moravianism in England is Fulneck, in Yorkshire.

[2] Modern Moravians disclaim all connection with the adherents of Hutter.

at Frankenhaussen, mentioned in the previous chapter, settled in Moravia to escape what they called the servitude of Egypt, and to take possession, as the elect people of God, of the Land of Promise. They established a community of goods without falling into the gross errors of the Anabaptists, and were distinguished from other sectaries of the times by the purity of their manners and the earnestness of their religious convictions. Hutter himself was a Cromwell on a small scale. He felt that Communism could only exist under severe and inflexible laws, administered by an authority purely religious, accepted freely yet exercised despotically. None but men of blameless lives and devout characters were admitted into the community, and, thanks to the administrative skill of this firm and austere leader, and the richness of the district he had selected as the scene of his operations, the success of the settlement was complete. A number of similar communities sprang up stimulated by this success, and less prolific soils were occupied and turned into valuable properties by the exertions of the Brethren. The settlements bore pretty much the same character throughout. Palisades marked the boundary of each colony, cottages for separate households were built within the enclosure, and in the middle (as in Fourier's imagined *Phalanstère*[1]) were erected the public buildings for general purposes, comprehending a common refectory, magazines, workshops, and schoolrooms. Parents were relieved of the care of their children, who were given into the charge of widows of an advanced age. An *Economist*, charged with the revenues and disbursements of the colony, was chosen annually by the brotherhood. Meals were taken together and in silence. Food was frugal, and the clothing and furniture of the simplest kind, and uniform in appearance. Work was done noiselessly, and feasts and festivals were totally abolished. The Brethren were subjected to a severe discipline under the absolute rule of the *Archimandrite*, who, as to his office and powers, strongly resembled the Grand Metaphysician suggested in Campanella's " City of the Sun."

" The first rule " of the society, we are told, " was *not to suffer any idle persons among the Brethren*. From early morning, after prayers,

---

[1] The Phalanstery or Association is what Fourier considered the natural form of society, and that in which the human race would group in accordance with the laws of attraction and repulsion. It should consist of 400 families or 1800 persons, which number he found included the whole circle of human capacities. These should live in one immense edifice (the *Phalanstère*) in the centre of a well-cultivated domain, furnished with all the appliances of science and art, whether for purposes of industry or amusement. See a full account in the Author's work on Utopias, pp. 67–88.

which each performed in private, some dispersed over the fields to engage in agricultural labour, others were busy in the public workshops at the respective trades which they had been taught. No one was exempt from work of some sort. Thus, if a person of position had joined their ranks he was reduced, according to the Lord's injunction, to eat his bread in the sweat of his brow. . . . . All outward vices were banished from the society . . . None but spiritual weapons were employed to prevent or punish disorders . . . Public penance and exclusion from the Lord's Supper were punishments the most dreaded. The worst offenders were expelled from the communities and thrust back into the world."

Thus the society, living in peaceable retirement, and gaining the confidence of landed proprietors who gladly let their farms to people of such frugal habits and honest trustworthiness, made considerable progress, and was treated with considerable favour by the local authorities. It escaped almost entirely the persecution of the Protestants in the sixteenth century. Soon however internal dissensions and religious disputes undermined the foundations of the newly-formed communities, and they had to be dissolved. Many members returned to their original homes in Germany and Switzerland, where they became objects of public charity, so that the Senate of Zurich passed a decree that no more emigrations to the Moravian settlements should be allowed, since, to quote the words of the Act of the Legislative Assembly, "the emigrants returned to our States and became a burden to their relatives." A small remnant of the original settlers only survived. The last vestiges disappeared from the scene about the year 1620, when the bloody persecutions of the Protestants, by order of Ferdinand II of Austria, exterminated this as well as the other branch of the Moravian Church next to be considered.

This body, better known as the *Unitas Fratrum*, sprung from the remnant of persecuted Hussites. Permission was given to them by the reigning sovereign to retire to the lordship of Lititz, on the confines of Moravia and Silesia, and there to establish a colony with liberty to introduce their own peculiar worship and discipline. The numbers increased rapidly. It was recruited by citizens of Prague, members of the learned professions, and the nobility from Bohemia and Moravia. The title, "Fratres legis Christi[1]" was at first assumed, but as this seemed to convey the idea of a monastic order it was soon exchanged for that of "Unitas Fratrum,"

[1] Marsden, "Dictionary of Christian Churches and Sects," i. p. 103.

or the United Brethren. This was in 1457. Ten years later the Church was finally established at the Synod of Lotha, when three brethren, chosen by lot, were set apart for the ministry. These afterwards received Episcopal orders from their Waldensian brethren who had found refuge in Austria during the persecutions we have mentioned in a previous chapter. External pressure, in the form of Government measures for the suppression of the sect, only cemented their union, and such was the reverential regard in which they were held by the outer world, owing to their personal virtue and the signal Divine protection accorded them in the midst of persecution, that a proverb became current—" If any one is tired of life, let him lay hands on the Picards " (a nickname of the Moravians).

In the year 1500 the number of their parishes was about 200, and the communities were strictly under ecclesiastical government, whilst a common fund provided for all the emergencies of expenditure, whether ecclesiastical or secular. The elders watched over the moral purity of the society, and had the power to banish any members convicted of vicious habits. There is however no proof of the actual establishment among them of a community of goods either at that time or at any later period of their eventful history.

On the contrary, we are assured by Mr. Holmes in his " History of the United Brethren," that nothing like a community of goods exists in any of the Moravian settlements, although it is expected " that all the inhabitants will take a voluntary share, according to their ability, in defraying the necessary public expenses, and as good citizens be amenable to the municipal regulations of the settlement[1]." The friendly relations which had been established between the United Brethren and the Protestant Churches in the Germanic Empire subjected them, especially the brethren in Bohemia, to the usual pains and penalties. They found a temporary exile in Poland and Prussia, where they established a new branch of the society. Their final expulsion took place six years after the persecution mentioned already, in 1621, when their last Bishop, Comenius, who had been a preacher at Fulneck, in Moravia, which is, so to speak, the sacred Mecca of the United Brethren, left the country. After living in exile in various lands, and for a time in England, he returned to Amsterdam, where he died in 1670.

Nearly a century passed away before we hear

---

[1] Holmes, "History of the Protestant Churches of the United Brethren," vol. i. p. 253. This refers to later settlements, but is equally applicable to the earlier ones.

again of the Brethren, who seemed to have become extinct. Some of them however remained here and there in secrecy and retirement, keeping up the continuity of their religious and social institutions. Great political convulsions disturbed Europe during this period. The horrors of the Thirty Years' War devastated and depopulated Germany; the Great Rebellion, the Restoration, and the Second Revolution passed over England; and in France the concentration of power in the hands of the monarch succeeded those religious and social struggles, such as the League and the *Fronde*, which had followed in the wake of the Reformation. Thus the foremost nations of Europe were prostrate and exhausted. Monarchical absolutism laid its heavy hand on the oppressed people, who had neither the will nor the power to oppose encroachments upon their liberties and property. A royal marriage united Saxony and France. Madame de Pompadour, a minion of the king, ruled in the French capital. Brühl, an unprincipled minister, was all-powerful at the court of Saxony. Heavy and unjust taxation ground down the people in both countries. Murmurs of discontent were silenced behind dungeon walls, where the malcontents were incarcerated sometimes for life. A noble-minded Saxon, Count Zinzendorf, disgusted with these enormities in high places, left his post of honour in the council chamber, and sought for peace of mind away from the vices of society, by withdrawing to the quiet hamlet of *Herrnhut*[1], built by Christian David in 1722, an asylum for himself and others likeminded. The remnant of the Brethren left in Bohemia and Moravia joined him, and thus was formed the nucleus of the new society of the United Brethren, whose settlements now extend over almost every part of the habitable globe.

This settlement at its commencement was intended as a standing protest against the corruptions of civil life and the decadence of true religion in Germany. The rigidity of formal religion was gradually undermining Protestantism as it had before deadened the religious life of the Catholic Church. A new reformation in Church and State was needed to meet coldness and indifference in sacred things as well as injustice and oppression in secular matters. Pious Mysticism and Christian Socialism, so often found together, revived as they had done in the pre-Reformation period, and protested against corruption in Church and State. Zinzendorf, with his school of pilgrims traversing the Old and New World to make converts to his principles of spiritual religion and social simplicity, recalls to our mind the efforts of the Beghards

---

[1] It means ' The Lord's protection.'

and the Fratricelli, the Lollards and the Apostolici of an earlier age.

"At court," says Zinzendorf, referring to his removal to Herrnhut, "I have resembled Mordecai, and I did not always find it easy to make ministerial firmness agree with the meekness of a disciple of Christ, and this has been a hindrance to my advance in the religion of the heart. Sometimes when I ought to have sought for victory by patient endurance, I have endeavoured to obtain it by making use of my civil prerogatives; but I have not always succeeded. Other and greater sufferings, such as have befallen my brethren, may await me in future; but I lay aside the armour of Saul, and choose Him for my defence who gave strength to the shepherd's boy [1]."

Inspired by such sentiments, we see Zinzendorf devoting all his energies to the new cause, and undergoing hardships, trials, and disappointments, as zealous in his spiritual apostleship as St. Paul, as active as Robert Owen in his attempts at social reform. Now we find him among the doctors at Tübingen endeavouring to gain recognition for his people as an orthodox community; then at Copenhagen to get the royal patronage for his missions; now holding conferences with the Archbishop of Canter-

[1] Holmes, "History of United Brethren," vol. i. p. 235.

bury; then discoursing before Berlin assemblies; one day suddenly appearing among the German settlers in Pennsylvania, and on another before the chiefs of the Red Indians on the Susquehannah, everywhere organising and extending his new society. Returning from time to time to Herrnhut to put things in order and to overcome financial difficulties, he continued his labour of love until 1760, when he passed away. As he completed his last work, the revision of the " Daily Words," he handed it over to his amanuensis with the remark, " Now rest is sweet [1]."

The constitution of the Moravian Brethren since the death of their second founder has undergone some alterations in favour of self-government. There has been a gradual and peaceful change from ecclesiastical imperialism to democratic ecclesiasticism, or the rule of spiritual heads by means of popular suffrage. As economic difficulties called for a more representative form of government, and the rapid spread of the society in all parts of the world made implicit obedience to a central authority more difficult and irksome, provincial synods and local self-government were introduced in addition to the general synod of the whole body. Moreover, the three great revolutions in

[1] Cranz, "Modern History of the Brethren," p. 493.

France, with their influences on the social conditions of other European countries, could not fail to produce some effect, even on a society of this kind, living apart from the rest of mankind in a semi-religious social seclusion. The progress of democracy among the Herrnhuters kept time with the same movement in the outer world, gradually changing their government from personal rule to a collegiate administration, from centralisation to decentralisation, and with every crisis introducing new reforms in the directory. Thus the society was preserved from splitting up into separate communities by according autonomy to all without unloosening the common bond of union between them [1].

---

[1] Perhaps the chief cause of the remarkable success of the Moravian Society is its aptitude to unite with other Christian bodies. Unlike many other churches, it seldom offends those opposed to it in principle, but holds out the right hand of fellowship to all. The effect of this policy can be seen in the still flourishing settlements of the Moravians in the United States. Their principal settlement at Bethlehem in Pennsylvania was originally founded by David Nitschman, one of the companions of Count Zinzendorf, who arrived there from Europe in 1740 with a company of brethren and sisters. "The place," says the historian Loskiel, "was wild and woody, at a distance of eighty miles from the nearest town, and only two European houses stood in the neighbourhood, about two miles up the river. No other dwellings were to be seen in the whole country except the scattered huts or cottages of the Indians." Years of difficulty and danger followed, as

Although not actually Communists, the
United Brethren in their social organisation
aimed at comparative equality[1]. Several hundred
individuals often lived in the same building,
having a common kitchen and dining-room.
The produce of their labour was thrown into a
common stock, and distributed by fiscal authorities elected by the community from among
its members. The stewards and elders of the

the settlement was close to the old Indian trail going north-
wards from Philadelphia, and was at the southern extremity
of that district rendered famous by Cooper in his Indian
tales. The brethren bravely sustained their position, and survived the still greater danger brought by advancing civilisation, and the development of the internal resources of the
district in the shape of an unsympathic and even adverse
immigration. The old practice of living in choirs according
to sex and state has been long discontinued, and the community has been gradually brought into harmony with the
surrounding population.

The author is indebted for the information contained in
this note to Mr. William F. Bailey, B.A., Barrister-at-Law,
Hon. Sec. Statistical and Social Inquiry Society of Ireland,
who has quite lately visited the place described.

It is only just to mention in this place, too, the great obligation of the author to Mr. Bailey for his painstaking efforts
in revising the sheets of this book while passing through the
press, and for many valuable hints made use of in the present publication.

[1] " Comparative Equality" is aimed at, only to some extent
now among the United Brethren, solely in spiritual matters,
and touches secular relations only in so far as is at once
desirable and inevitable." Quoted from a private communication from a Moravian authority.

brotherhood chosen to this office have charge of all secular matters, and are responsible to the general assemblies for the proper discharge of their trust. The people, as a rule, are divided into choirs, according to sex and state. There are choirs of youths and maidens, of husbands and wives, of widowers and widows. Maidens, wives, and widows are distinguished by the colour of their ribbons.

Education is common, and all are treated as members of the same family. All work at some calling and none are idle. Accumulation of capital is rendered practically impossible, since the superfluities of the more wealthy are expected to be devoted to the wants of the needy. Want, accordingly, is unknown, and undue differences between rich and poor are lessened by the exercise of Christian charity.

Marriages are contracted with scrupulous care, and are unaffected by mercenary considerations. There is no strong tendency towards celibacy among the brethren, as the training and maintenance of the children are provided for by public institutions. The Moravians in many respects resemble the Essenes. Their differences correspond to the distinctive peculiarities which separate Judaism from Christianity. There is less asceticism among the Moravians, and their social arrangements and the physiological basis on which they rest might be called St. Simonian on strictly Christian principles[1]. In fact, religious principles are the guide of life, and the dissemination of the Christian religion is the bond of union between the several societies of Moravians all over the world. Social arrangements are considered of importance only as means to this end. Accordingly we find that every wave of scepticism which has passed over Europe and diminished religious enthusiasm has had a considerable effect on the growth and condition of the society. About the middle of the eighteenth century it counted 70,000 members; in 1852 Thonissen, in his history of Socialism, estimated the number at 18,000 only. According to latest official returns, examined by the present writer,

[1] St. Simon, born in Paris in 1760, was the propagator of extremely revolutionary and democratic doctrines, though reared "in a perfect hot-bed of aristocratic prejudice." After undergoing many vicissitudes of fortune, he died in 1825, leaving to his disciples (of whom Comte was chief) the working out of his philosophical theories. "The St. Simonian scheme does not contemplate," says Mill, "an equal but an unequal division of the produce; it does not propose that all should be occupied alike, but differently, according to their vocation or capacity; the function of each being assigned, like grades in a regiment, by the choice of the directing authority, and the remuneration being by salary, proportioned to the importance, in the eyes of that authority, of the function itself, and the merit of the person who fulfils it."—*Principles of Political Economy*, Bk. II. Chap. II. 4.

there has been an increase upon this, the total number being 30,969[1], an increase which may be attributed to the revival of religious life in the last quarter of the present century. The general prosperity of the society, again, is greatly dependent on the spirit of Christian self-denial and devotion to the missionary cause which exists among them. "What furnished the Church with such abundant resources," says one of its historians, " was that no one thought of living to himself, but only for the Lord and His Church. Everywhere might be witnessed a severe temperance; all were prepared to be satisfied with the most frugal fare, narrow house accommodation, and furniture of the most simple kind. Clothing was equally simple, etc. . . . . In a word, the *love of poverty*, side by side with continued labour, in which children were taught to share from an early age, trust and thankfulness towards God, joined to acts of charity towards the Brethren, such were the sources of comparative wealth, so that no one lacked the necessaries of life, while no one enjoyed any superfluities. If any one sought external ease and comfort, or wished to amass [property], not being disposed to follow the Saviour in His poverty and holiness, such a

---

[1] I. e. irrespective of 76,642 members in the various missions belonging to the body.

one could soon discover that he was not fit to remain a member of the society [1]."

In fact, since the year 1727, the society has continued to be a community of " brethren " in the apostolic sense of the word, religiously and socially. Private property is not abolished, but to a certain extent the apostolic obligation of contributing towards the common fund, without establishing pure Communism, remains the binding law of the Society.

The same may be said of the zeal for missions, which recalls the wonderful efforts and successes of the Primitive Church. The first missionaries left for " Greenland's icy mountains " in 1733. Others followed in rapid succession, until Labrador and Indiana, the West Indies, South America, and even Australia, were visited in turn. Negroes and Bushmen, Hindoos and Hottentots, received the Divine message from Moravian missionaries and evangelists. At the same time home missions in Europe were not neglected, and the religious ardour of the Brethren was communicated to other religious bodies by emissaries sent forth for that purpose.

---

[1] A. Bost, " Histoire Ancienne et Moderne de l'Eglise des Frères de Bohème et de Moravie," tome ii. p. 15. This interesting work may be had in an English Translation published at the office of the Society, 42 Berners Street, Oxford Street, W.

At the present moment about 76,642 persons are under missionary influence, and thousands of children and young people of various ages are educated in the schools and colleges of the Moravian missions abroad [1].

The temporal progress and social improvement of the peoples among whom the Brethren work are attended to as well as their spiritual welfare. The benefits of civilisation are taught, so that the condition of the converted heathen soon surpasses in outward prosperity and peaceable government that of the unconverted tribes around them [2].

" Along the whole extent of the western coast of Greenland the barbarities of savage life, and the enormities attending paganism, where dominant, are rarely to be met with," wrote Mr. Holmes in 1827; " and the state of this country, compared with what it was eighty, or but fifty years ago, may be called civilised. The nature and climate of this dreary region, no less than the methods by which the natives must procure their subsistence, necessarily preclude the introduction of most of the useful

---

[1] See " Brief Historical Sketch of the Missions," published Aug. 21st, 1882. Also " The Moravian Almanack " for 1883.

[2] See Spangenberg's " Account of the Manner in which the Protestant Churches of the Unitas Fratrum preach the Gospel," etc., p. 102.

arts of civilised society. They can neither till the land nor engage in manufactures. The power is denied them by the sterility of the rocks they inhabit, and the rigours of the polar sky; and the latter, with very few exceptions, are, for the same reasons, rendered useless. But it may be said with truth, that the converted Greenlanders, by their habits of industry, which they have acquired since the introduction of the gospel among them, by their contentment amidst many privations and hardships, and by the charity of the more affluent of their needy brethren, strikingly exemplify the doctrine of the great Apostle of the Gentiles, that in every circumstance of life and in every nation, *God-liness is great gain, having the promise of the life that now is, and of that which is to come* [1]."

We may indeed apply to these primitive societies the praise bestowed on the Moravians in Hungary by an English traveller as far back as 1659, that they are " an honest, simple-hearted people, humble, godly, laborious, well trained up, and lovers of discipline."

The late Mr. Wilberforce, in his well-known work on " Practical Christianity," speaks of the Moravian missionaries as " a body of Christians who have, perhaps, excelled all mankind in solid

[1] Holmes, "Historical Sketches of the Missions of the United Brethren," p. 64.

and unequivocal proofs of the love of Christ, and of the most ardent, active, and patient zeal in His service.   It is a zeal," he continues, " tempered with prudence, softened with meekness, soberly aiming at great ends by the gradual operation of well adapted means, supported by a courage which no danger can intimidate, and quiet constancy which no hardship can exhaust."   The missions to Greenland, to Labrador, to the American Indians, to the negroes of the West Indies, and to the natives of Southern Africa, although the chief, are not the only efforts of the Moravian Church. A mission to the aborigines of Australia was established twenty-three years ago (1859), and another was commenced in Thibet, to the Mongol tribes, a little earlier (1854).   Each of these missions may be regarded as a kind of outpost of the Christian Church in the wilds of heathenism.   Indeed, it is the occupying of outposts such as these that has been the greatest and most honourable work of the Moravian Brethren.

M. Villegardelle cites with approval a plan of M. Faiguet's in Diderot's " Encyclopædia " for the gradual reconstruction of society on the Moravian system.   M. Faiguet mentions the survival of some ancient families of labourers in Auvergne, who, he says, might be called the

Moravians of France. Their mode of life resembles in all essential respects that of the Moravian brethren, a short and necessarily imperfect sketch of which has been already presented to the reader. The question suggests itself whether the social arrangements of the Moravians could be adapted to society at large, and if so, whether their success has been such as would render the experiment advisable.

We have seen how religious fanaticism and theological differences brought about the dissolution of that branch of the Moravians among whom the most thorough-going Communism prevailed. We have seen also how religious fervour, in its most simple form, has all along been the main source of strength in the still existing branch, the success of which, numerically and financially, has depended entirely on the rigour and purity of the religious life. The abatement, therefore, of religious ardour, or the development of religious animosities, might at any time prove a serious danger to the society. How, then, could any large body of human beings, say a nation or aggregate of nations, be held together socially, in the presence of religious differences and the animosities they are sure to engender among its component members?

But suppose these difficulties could be overcome and the " enthusiasm of humanity " relied

on by modern speculators could replace religious
ardour, it would still remain a doubtful pro-
position whether the civilisation and contented
simplicity of the Moravians is the highest possible condition to be sought for by social reformers. Has their general culture and mental
development reached that height of perfection
which we, in this age of refined intellectualism,
regard as the highest ideal? Has progress in
the arts and sciences, and the enlightened
toleration which accompanies such advancement, been the distinguishing mark of this
excellent society? What would happen if their
patriarchal simplicity became the general rule
for all mankind? Retrogression rather than progress would be the result. The dull monotony of
life, deprived of that which embellishes and gives
the charm of novelty and variety to existence,
would soon become insupportable. The regular
tread of the companies of workers proceeding
day after day to their labour in mute self-absorp-
tion, acquitting themselves of the task rigorously
assigned to them by authority; the uniformity of
sombre dress and furniture, with its oppressive influence on the senses; and the passive
obedience to orders, without the exercise of
spontaneity and individual discovery, would
deaden the mental activities and reduce the
rational creature to the condition of a self-acting

machine. Even the softer emotions of love and friendship in the natural selection of the sexes would be reduced to system, or left to chance. All this, so far from ameliorating the condition of humanity, would only substitute other social evils for those already existing, and cast a sadness and a gloom over human hearts unrelieved by those rays of a better hope, and unsoftened by those higher aspirations of the spiritual life, which now console the Moravian Brethren in the midst of voluntary privations, and in the absence of the varied enjoyments of a cultured society.

Whilst, then, we cannot help admiring the piety, the moral grandeur, the self-denial, and the fortitude of character to be found among this simple-minded people, we cannot help noticing, on the other hand, that it has not produced as yet any real genius; that its social status has never passed the point of respectable mediocrity; that its literary and scientific attainments are not of a high order; that as a society it has never risen above the low level of ordinary competency. Such being the case, the past history and present condition of the Moravian communities may serve, indeed, as a practical example of simple contentedness to our modern society in its

insatiable thirst after luxurious indulgence.
They may serve as models of self-devotion to
the common cause in an age of egotistical ma-
terialism, as guides for those who seek to bring
about social regeneration on a moral basis; but
while human nature remains as it is, the social
organisation of the Moravians, as a whole, can
never serve as a pattern for the reconstruction
of the society of the future[1].

[1] By an imperial decree of the Austro-Hungarian Government, published in 1880, the body under the name of
" Evangelical Brethren's Church " has been recognised, and
several additional congregations have been formed in the
country. Otherwise no marked changes have taken place in
the historical development of the community. Its expansive
power is evidenced, however, by the following statistics,
quoted from the Moravian Almanack, 1883, giving the present condition of the churches founded, and their missions :—

GENERAL CHURCH STATISTICS.

I. MEMBERS—	Communicants.	Total.
German Province (26 Congregations) about	5,882	8,003
,, ,, Diaspora and other Agents on the Continent	115	170
British ,, (38 Congregations, including Home Missions) ..	3,220	5,645
American, Northern Province (53 Congregations, including Home Missions) ..	8,362	14,372
American, Southern Province (6 Congregations, including Home Missions) ..	1,292	2,133
Bohemia	156	246
Missions (16 Provinces)	25,984	76,642
Missionaries and families in various parts of the world	315	400
	45,326	107,611

II. SUNDAY SCHOOLS—	Scholars.	Teachers.
British Province	3,996	597
American, Northern	7,494	921
,, Southern	1,043	94
	12,533	1.612

III. BOARDING SCHOOLS—

						Pupils.	Schools.
German Province	..	..	..	about		1,050	25
British	„	..	..	..	..	502	14
American	„	N. and S.	..	..		300	5
						1,852	44

IV. DAY SCHOOLS—

						Pupils.	Schools.
German Province	..	..	..	about		1,220	36
British	„	..	..	..	..	1,131	11
						2,351	47

Most of the American and some of the English Day Schools have been merged into Government or Board Schools. It is computed that 70,000 souls are in connection with our Diaspora on the Continent of Europe.

The number of souls under Moravian teaching may be thus summed up :—

In the Home Congregations of the three Provinces	..	..	30,969
„ Foreign Missions	.. ..	..	76,642
„ Diaspora	.. ..	..	70,000
„ Schools, Boarding, Day and Sunday	..	..	16,736
	Total	.. ..	194,347

NUMERICAL STATISTICS OF MISSIONS, JULY, 1882.

MISSION PROVINCES.	Stations.	Missionary Agents.	Native Ministers and Assistants.	Native Helpers and occasional Assistants.	Communicants.	Baptized Adults.	Candidates, New People, &c.	Baptized Children.	TOTAL.
Greenland . .	6	21	—	61	775	106	243	454	1578
Labrador . .	6	39	—	48	506	344	—	448	1298
N. A. Indians .	4	8	—	11	118	51	18	144	331
Jamaica . . .	15	26	4	267	5336	2949	264	6901	15,450
St. Thomas . .	3	4	—	30	1016	129	83	469	1697
St. Jan . . .	2	—	1	26	371	69	14	304	758
St. Croix . .	3	4	1	51	1201	129	99	499	1928
Antigua . . .	8	11	7	161	3174	1331	273	2440	7218
St. Kitts . . .	4	4	4	70	1593	844	201	1329	3967
Barbados . .	4	2	4	65	1348	382	73	1371	3174
Tobago . .	3	4	1	58	1186	416	68	1169	2839
Demerara . .	2	—	4	5	124	56	—	104	284
Moskito Coast .	7	12	3	23	248	357	482	624	1711
Surinam . . .	14	68	—	353	6201	6768	2671	6913	22,553
S. Africa West	7	41	4	231	2157	1616	2006	3511	9290
S. Africa East	7	20	2	64	592	189	872	761	2414
Australia. . .	2	6	—	—	23	2	39	54	118
Tibet	2	7	—	—	15	3	—	16	34
	99*	277	35	1524	25,984	15,741	7406	27,511	76,642

* There are also 16 filials or out-stations.

CHAPTER VI.

THE CHRISTIAN REPUBLIC AT PARAGUAY.

OUR survey of Utopian experiments would be incomplete did we not devote some attention to a remarkable community founded in South America on the principles of equality, but subject to an enlightened despotism. We have passed in review several Communistic experiments which have invariably ended in failure. In all these cases the rulers and the ruled were originally of the same race, and in most instances belonged to the same social class. The case is different with the Commonwealth of Equals established in Paraguay, where the natives were reduced from a state of semi-savage independence under the complete management of a highly civilised paternal government.

> " When the happier sons of Paraguay,
>   By gentleness and pious art subdued,
>   Bowed their meek heads beneath the Jesuits' sway
>   And lived and died in filial servitude."

In tracing the history of this remarkable

society, which has been held up as a pattern of good government and national content-ment by such high authorities as Muratori and Montesquieu[1], we shall have occasion to note the effects of communistic principles applied by a superior race, in a religious spirit, to a people just emerging from barbarism. At the same time we shall have an opportunity of dis-tinguishing the social tendencies of Romanism and Protestantism respectively, in a comparison of the Moravian and Jesuit settlements. These, although they differ widely in the manner of their foundation, development, and final results, have this in common, that both start with the identical object of promoting a higher religious life on an improved social basis, that basis being Christian equality.

At the time the Pilgrim Fathers left their native land to settle in the Far West, a band of Jesuit Missionaries had already succeeded in founding a new Christian society in the New World.

Almost the same year which gave the death-blow to the ancient Moravian Brotherhood in Bohemia marked the complete success of the Jesuits in Paraguay, twenty-one settlements

[1] Even Voltaire, the sworn enemy of the Jesuits, says: "The establishment in Paraguay of the Spanish Jesuits alone, seems, in some respects, to be the triumph of hu-manity."

having sprung into existence during almost as many years' labour of the Fathers. But how different are the results! Whilst from New England the North American continent has been peopled with an ever-advancing race, vieing in the spirit of enterprise and progress with the foremost nations of the Old World, the South American Republics, and Paraguay among them, are still in a backward state of civilisation. While, as we saw in the last chapter, the Moravians have developed into an influential confederacy, conducting successful missions for the social and religious emancipation of the whole human race, the Jesuit *Misiones*, in the Indian Commonwealth of Paraguay, have entirely disappeared, and the work so promising and successful for a time has given place to ruin and desolation. Is it too much to infer from this, as has M. Emile de Laveleye, an eminent Belgian economist and himself an enlightened Romanist, in comparing the social condition of Protestant and Catholic nations generally, " that Protestants advance more rapidly and steadily than Catholics," so that it is " difficult not to attribute the superiority of the one over the other to the religion they profess [1] ? "

[1] See his pamphlet, " Protestantism and Catholicism in their bearing upon the Liberty and Prosperity of Nations,"

Perhaps an answer to this question may be found in the history of the settlement itself, and to this we shall now direct the reader's attention.

A fertile soil, irrigated by two noble rivers and their tributaries, no great difficulties of transit, owing to the absence of lofty mountains, navigable rivers encouraging inland communication, abundant variety in native produce, and wood in plenty for building both houses and ships—such were the natural conditions of the country all favourable to the social experiments of the invaders. The natives themselves, of a gentle and docile disposition, to a certain extent the result of their mild and genial surroundings, were easily made amenable to religious instructors, and perhaps rendered prone to superstition, by awe-inspiring natural phenomena, such as terrible thunderstorms and lightning. Averse to commercial enterprise in the absence of the indispensable requisites of industrial activity, they retained a natural simplicity and a hospitable and even generous disposition, though somewhat wanting in moral fibre and vigorous independence. Such were the people selected by the Jesuits for spiritual conquest and for social experiment as a means for promoting that

translated, with a Preface, by the Right Hon. W. E. Gladstone, M.P., p. 11, *et passim.*

end. Let us now see how they went to work in order to attain it.

It was towards the end of the sixteenth century that the first settlements, or "Reductions," were organised on the fertile plains of Uruguay, east of Paraguay, in a sheltered position encircled by chains of mountains sufficiently high to preserve the settlers from the incursions of unruly neighbours[1]. The salubrity of the soil and brightness of the atmosphere gave every promise of ultimate success. Here the missionaries collected the scattered bands of natives who had been roaming in forests and living in caverns, strangers to the pleasures of home and the security and sweet enjoyments of a civilised life. They changed their habits from the predial to the peaceful state, and turned their attention from the chase to agricultural pursuits. They began by providing food and shelter, and established a guild of weavers to manufacture European stuffs for clothing the natives. They opened an apothecary's shop, a public library, and educational establishments to instruct their new converts in the principles of religion and the arts of life.

[1] The Spaniards first settled in the country in 1515. The Jesuit Mission was established in 1608, and expelled in 1768. In 1811 Paraguay was freed from Spanish rule, and in 1817 Dr. Francia became Dictator of the Republic. Its independence was recognised by Great Britain in 1853.

They encouraged native industry and taught the rudiments of a commercial system applied to inland traffic, and they established agencies for the exportation of goods, the Procurator-General acting as the sole medium in all commercial transactions with the outer world. This was done professedly with a view to avoid the evils of the mercantile system in Europe, with its corrupting influence on morals and its tendency to bring about social degeneration. At the same time the Jesuits carefully preserved the natives from the temptations of competition among themselves by establishing a community of goods. By means of pious frauds they gained a powerful ascendency over the native mind, and by a careful and just distribution of the necessaries and comforts of life, the result of associated work, they secured their affection and admiration.

> " Benevolence had gained such empire there,
> That even superstition had been brought
> An aspect of humanity to wear,
> And make the weal of man its first and only care."

Their zealous anxiety for the temporal and spiritual welfare of the converts, and their frequent exhibition of self-denial, often incurring dangers and undergoing sufferings on their behalf, raised them in general esteem. The area of their activity was soon extended, and the number of adherents increased, so that within fifty years of their landing on the coast of Brazil, they had gathered around them no less than 100,000 natives, spread over about thirty settlements. Each settlement had a town of simple but not unsightly mud houses, whitened and covered with tiles, and provided with verandahs on either side. Every mission had its own church, generally built of stone, and magnificently ornamented. Two curates were attached to each of these, who were required to fill the offices of parochial minister as well as general organiser of the local government and social economy. Thus the Jesuits became at once the teachers and the magistrates of the community.

To protect their followers from the incursions of the lawless settlers in the neighbouring province of St. Paul, they trained them in the art of self-defence and fortification, as they had previously taught them habits of industry. Romantic accounts of the heroic defences of the settlers when attacked by overpowering numbers of these ruthless freebooters and marauders, called " Mamelukes," are related in the history of the *Misiones*. The ecclesiastical governors thus had frequent opportunities to distinguish themselves by a noble fearlessness in the midst of danger, and a devoted self-forgetfulness in their endeavour to save the commonwealth from the terror and scourge of powerful enemies, and thus enhanced still more the love and reverence of the people for them[1]. The zeal of the pastors increased the fervour of devotion among the people.

The religious exercises forming part of their regular routine, resembled, in a measure, those of the Moravians under similar conditions, of course making due allowance for the differences of religious dogma and ceremonial usage in the two bodies. The following is a description by Muratori: "Every morning, before dawn, the children go to church, taking their place there, girls on one side, boys on the other. There they recite prayers and creeds until the rising of the sun. Then follows the mass, in which all the inhabitants must join, except in particular cases demanding dispensation. After this, everybody goes to work. In the evening the children are catechised. Then the bell summons all the faithful to vespers. Special services on Sundays and on other occasions preserve the religious tone of the people, and churc discipline, strict, though gentle, preserves the community from worldliness and

---

[1] See, for an interesting and detailed account of a typical case of the kind, "Letters on Paraguay," by J. P. and W. P. Robertson, vol. ii. p. 60, and following.

conduct unworthy the Christian profession. The sexes are kept apart in public places, and marriages are arranged not by mutual attachment, nor, as in the case of the Moravians, by casting lots and leaving the decision to Heaven, but by ecclesiastical authority acting for the community. Still, the results were, upon the whole, satisfactory. Chastity, soberness, and calm, peaceful enjoyment of life prevailed among the people of Paraguay. The cultivation of music and the dance at festivals, martial processions and tournaments, with prizes for the victors, provided innocent amusements. Religious pageants on special occasions were held to satisfy the craving for novelty and sensuous enjoyment among the people, and to keep before their eyes symbols of higher ideals. A perfect system of organised charity to relieve the distressed in their own community or strangers without it needing assistance, stimulating the virtue of self-denial, gave full play for the emotions of love and pity. Everything, in fact, we are told, was done to preserve an equal balance of mind and health of body, while the dictates of morality and religion are obeyed without murmur." In fact, the people of Paraguay, if we may give credence to Muratori, whom Gibbon speaks of as a " diligent and laborious writer, who aspires above the prejudices of the Catholic priest [1]," fulfilled most of the conditions of Lord Bacon's "New Atlantis" and Campanella's "City of the Sun" about the time those dreamy compositions were compiled. This was a strange coincidence of theory and practice in the Old and New World in thus contemporaneously working out Utopian ideals and social experiments. It gave expression to the spirit of the times which constantly sought to bring about an entire moral and material reformation among the masses of mankind.

It has to be noted, however, that although the principles of fraternal union and devotion to the common good, in imitation of the *naïve* simplicity of Primitive Christianity, proved the rule of life among the people of Paraguay, community of goods was more in the nature of a custom than a law, and therefore not rigorously enforced. Every one had his own field and herd of cattle. But in addition to *private* property there was also a *collective* or corporate property for the benefit of all, called *God's possession*. The products of this common property went towards paying the

---

[1] The aspirations of the Roman Catholic priest have, however, not always been realised, for the account he gives of the "Reductions" is undoubtedly tinged with partiality and a strong desire to defend the Jesuits at all hazards.

royal tribute due to the King of Spain, to provide for the exigencies of war and famine, and for the maintenance of members of the commonwealth when in distress, or afflicted by infirmities. All, even the heads of the towns, had to work, for "the community," at the bidding of their ecclesiastical rulers. Although the government was ostensibly in the hands of a representative body chosen by the people, implicit obedience to "catholic discipline," *i. e.*, the word of command of their spiritual superiors, was expected in this "Christian Republic." The rule thus imposed upon the Indians being upon the whole wise, humane, and beneficent, they wore their chains, which were almost imperceptible to their simple and guileless minds, without a murmur, unconscious that their uniform and constant labour, whilst contributing to their own support according to the comparatively low standard of life among them, was mainly instrumental in promoting the aggrandisement of the religious order to which their spiritual benefactors belonged.

While some apologists have endeavoured to represent the Jesuits as more disinterested and philanthropic than they actually were in their relation towards the natives, others have gone to the opposite extreme in attributing nothing but false motives to the schemes of these " refined rogues," as Dr. Francia, the Dictator of Paraguay, afterwards called them.

" Affecting to govern all their establishments on the principle of community of goods," say the authors of " Letters on Paraguay," "and having persuaded the Indians that they participated equally with their pastors in the advantages derived from their labour in common, the Jesuits made subservient to their own aggrandisement the toil of 100,000 Indian slaves. They instructed them in agriculture and in the mechanical arts; they made of them soldiers and sailors; and they taught them to herd cattle, prepare yerba, and manufacture sugar and cigars. But while the churches and casas de residencia were built with elaborate splendour, the Indian architect and mason occupied mud hovels. While the padres had all the conveniences, and even luxuries, that could be furnished by the carpenter and upholsterer, and while the churches exhibited fine specimens of architecture, carving, and embroidery, the Indian workman had scarce a table and a chair, very seldom a bed, and never any other hanging or coverlet in his hovel than a coarse poncho. The Indians *made* shoes, but the padres *wore* them, and exported the surplus. . . It is true that the Indian was fed and clothed out of the common stock of produce, but so scantily and disproportionately that, while his earnings might amount to a hundred dollars a year, his food and raiment never cost one-half of that sum! He was allowed two days in the week, latterly three, in which to cultivate a small patch of ground for himself; but whatever this produced went in diminution of the supplies issued to him from the public stores. So that, after all, it came to the same thing. The 'community' (that is, of the padres) was still the gainer by the personal labour of the Indian[1]."

On the other hand, Muratori, anticipating in his "tract," without altogether contradicting, these statements of our modern travellers, draws a ravishing picture of the Utopian felicity enjoyed by the people of Paraguay under the Jesuit *régime*. "Regulated liberty, abundant supplies of all the necessaries of life, a tiny home, indeed, but large enough for all purposes; peace, union, concord—do not these constitute a people's happiness?" Then he expatiates on the blessings of equality: "Caciques, captains, and magistrates, and the principal persons in the community, are distinguished, indeed, from the people, but this distinction is not founded on large or more permanent possessions, nor wealth arising from commerce and industry.

[1] See *loc. cit.* pp. 47, 48.

K

And so it does not remove equality as among ourselves between nobles and commons, rich and poor, masters and servants, odious distinctions by which one portion of the human family becomes a lasting object of dislike and envy to the other [1]."

If the want, he argues, of mines and metals, iron and steel, retards social progress by placing impediments in the way of industry, the total absence of gold and silver and every sort of money—"these idols of cupidity"—is a salutary preservative against the crying evils of the capitalistic system which prevails in more advanced communities; for commerce consists among these simple people in barter and the exchange of commodities.

Indolence and improvidence are the natural faults of people in a low state of social culture. But the prodigal wastefulness of the natives was

---

[1] So Southey, in his interesting "Tale of Paraguay":—
" Content and cheerful Piety were found
   Within their humble walls.   From youth to age
   The simple dwellers paced their even round
   Of duty, not desiring to engage
   Upon the busy world's contentious stage,
   Whose ways they wisely had been train'd to dread.
   Their inoffensive lives in pupilage
   Perpetually, but peacefully, they led,
From all temptations saved, and sure of daily bread."

Canto iv. 6.

mitigated by the watchful superintendence of the European missionaries, and provision was made to insure the community against unforeseen calamities. Inspectors also were selected to take the supervision of the country districts, to stimulate and enforce exertion, and to prevent the indolent from sharing the advantages of common labour unless they contribute their proper share towards the creation of commodities. In all these duties the missionaries took the lead. Nobles by birth, and learned men fresh from the universities of Europe, might be seen acting as shepherds, masons, carpenters, and carrying on all manner of common trades, for the purpose of teaching and stimulating the natives, who gazed with confused bewilderment at the strange spectacle. The result of all these precautions and efforts to maintain a community of goods may be summed up in a few words : " The Indians are poor, and yet lack nothing. They maintain among themselves perfect equality, which is the strongest support of union and public tranquillity."

It is difficult to reconcile so many conflicting statements, but we must remember that in such cases friends are apt to be too indulgent in their criticism, while enemies are to a similar degree unjust. It is only by a process of weighing and sifting the evidence on both sides that we can arrive at an approximately true conclusion.

Probably the following is a tolerably correct and unvarnished account. "A Jesuit Reduction was a model of order and regularity; perfect uniformity was observed in its long comfortably-built rows of houses, and the small circuit of the towns offered every facility for preserving its domestic tranquillity, or insuring a ready defence against outside danger. The great square was the centre-point, the public resort and general rendezvous of the people; upon it were erected the church, the college, the arsenal, the stores, the workshops of carpenters, joiners, weavers, and smiths, together with other important public buildings, all assembled under the close and unsleeping vigilance of the Fathers. . . . The Reduction moved and had its being, as it were, with the precision of clockwork. The people prayed, toiled, ate, and slept so long and no longer; from one duty or employment they passed to another, like soldiers changing guard, *equally participating in the charges of the day, each one undergoing his measure of fatigue for the one and common family.* . . . The Indian laboured for his spiritual guardian, and looked to him for a material return."

These are the carefully balanced statements of an independent witness, the commander of the United States expedition in 1853–56. He concludes, after a careful survey of the efforts of the Jesuits' mission: "If there were nothing in the Jesuit rule to excite emulation, yet the natives lived happily under it, attained considerable civilisation, and relapsed rapidly into barbarism under the temporal and spiritual rule which replaced that of the Fathers[1]."

There can be no doubt that under the management of the Jesuits (whatever their motives may have been) the "Reductions" were in a highly prosperous condition, and that their expulsion produced among the bulk of the population feelings of regret and despair, and had for its immediate result the entire disorganisation of the community, which within thirty years was reduced to one-half of its original size. But neither the success of the settlement under Jesuit rule nor its collapse afterwards prove in any way the perfection of the system they adopted. Their signal success, no doubt, was owing to the adaptabiiity of their benevolent despotism to Indians in their savage state. Their distance from the seats of royal and papal authority at home rendered their power absolute; and the system of subordination to central authority adopted in the colony itself (in fact

[1] "La Plata, the Argentine Confederation, and Paraguay," by Thomas J. Page, U.S.N., p. 499 et seq.

a wise combination of Socialism and Cæsarism in their social politics—Socialism for the ruled, Cæsarism for the rulers) in effect placed the supreme power over every member of the community in the hands of the Jesuit Superior, who with a firm hand directed the whole from the seat of government at Candelaria. But though this system of centralisation proved the strongest point in the government of the settlement, it failed to render the governed permanently happy.

" You see, my friend," writes the impartial and enlightened governor of the province of Concepcion, (appointed in 1781), " that however excellent a *régime* this might be, if practised by a master by his pupils, as by a father towards his children in their nonage, it could never train or form a people to anything like knowledge or liberty. . . . When men acted upon this *régime*, and upon these principles of political economy, it cannot be a matter of surprise that in the course of 150 years, which it is since the establishments were formed, such immense wealth should have been found, as well in the churches as in that fund called 'The Fund of the Community.' For my part I am not astonished at this, when I consider the vast fertility of the province; the complete subjugation of the Indians; that they were absolutely shut out from all intercourse with the Spaniards; and that, knowing no other authority than that of the Jesuits, they became mere tools in their hands."

When, therefore, this controlling authority was removed [1], the whole elaborately-constructed scheme fell to pieces; and the maladministration of the Spanish governors, who without possessing the administrative power of the Jesuit rulers introduced a general system of spoliation and corruption, completed the final ruin of the settlement. When again this hateful yoke was

---

[1] During the flourishing period of the settlement the Jesuits were the supreme rulers under the nominal suzerainty of the Spanish Crown. When, however, an exchange of prisoners was effected between the Spaniards and the Portuguese, by means of which seven Reductions in Paraguay fell into the hands of the latter, the Jesuits, after all their attempts to prevent this exchange had proved futile, roused the natives to rebellion and civil war, and even called in French officers to head the insurgents. The war lasted several years, until, in 1756, the Indians were finally subdued by the united armies of Spain and Portugal under Gomez Freire de Andrada, Governor of Rio Janeiro. The natives were treated by the conquerors either like slaves or forced back into the forests and deserts whence the Jesuits had drawn them. The settlements, entirely deprived of the patriarchal government of the priests, after the final expulsion of the Jesuits in 1768 consequent upon their suppression in Europe, soon returned to their original condition. Thus the political contests between the civil governments and the Order of the Jesuits in Europe brought about an utter collapse of a most promising social experiment in the New World.

removed, the people, who had been held in a state of helpless tutelage for a century and a half, lacked the power of self-government, and the once splendid edifice of a Utopian Republic rapidly crumbled to pieces.

This decline is illustrated by the description of Candelaria, the chief town and the seat of government, given by travellers in 1839, as compared with the same city under the flourishing *régime* that formerly existed.

" Candelaria, under the Jesuits, had 3064 inhabitants ; they were now diminished to 700. It had a splendid church, richly ornamented, a capacious college, large gardens, and extensive *characas*, or cultivated grounds, around it. The church was now in a state of dilapidation, the rain was pouring in through many apertures of the roof, the walls were bare, and even the altar was uncovered by a cloth. Not having been whitewashed for years, the walls were not only bare, but black. From the damp parts of them, at not distant intervals, there oozed out a green mould, forming a soil, from which depended nettles and other noxious weeds. The college was pretty much in the same state, and what had once been a bricklaid patio, or quadrangle, was so completely covered with grass and weeds, that no trace of the original foundation was discoverable. As for the unweeded garden, 'things

rank and gross in nature possessed it merely.'
Every fruit-tree had been hewed down for
firewood. Of the original huts and cottages,
scarcely a third of the number was standing,
and of those that did remain there was no line
so little observable as the perpendicular. They
were awry, some leaning to one side, some inclined to another, and all indicating a speedy
intention of laying their bones and dust in
the lap of mother earth, and by the side of
the tenements that had already mouldered to
decay."

At such a melancholy sight the travellers
"almost regretted, upon the face of its dreari-
ness, depopulation, and decay, that the Jesuits
were not still its masters." In a postscript
to a later edition they add that since the above
was written the *Misiones* have been falling into
still greater ruin, year after year, so that
scarcely a vestige remains of what were once so
flourishing. The public buildings have crumbled
into decay ; the scattered inhabitants, almost
deprived of subsistence, wander about in
the woods. Their towns have been repeatedly
burned and sacked during revolutions, their
cattle have been destroyed or carried away.
Every trace of prosperity and cultivation has
disappeared, and the ruin of the Indians, like
the fall of the Jesuits, though not quite so

sudden, has been equally complete; it has been incalculably more calamitous.

What is the cause of this great difference between Paraguay "Past and Present?" It arises from grave errors in social politics and political economy on the part of the Jesuits. Community of goods weakens the motives for exertion and retards economic progress. The low level of mediocrity was rarely surpassed by the natives simply because there was no inducement offered for extra exertion. The men and women of the settlement did what the Fathers bid them do, and received with thankfulness the necessaries of life and scanty creature comforts in return, but nothing stirred them up into greater activity when their immediate wants had been supplied. The spiritual authority once removed, nothing but the slave-whip of Spanish Government inspectors would accelerate their movements, and when freed from this latter bondage their natural indolence and the insecurity of acquired possessions lamed every further effort toward industrial progress among the independent natives.

The principle of enlightened despotism, as applied to nations in a low state of civilisation, although at first often successful, becomes pernicious if adopted as a permanent measure.

" The practical result is," as Sir George Cornwall Lewis has pointed out, "that a community is least likely to obtain a good representative government when it is most wanted, and most likely to obtain one when it is least wanted[1]." This is exactly what happened in the case of the people under consideration. The Jesuits, jealous of their power, discouraged representative government, and consequently purposely retarded the political education of the people. They would not allow them to advance beyond the stage of tutelage. The consequence was that when the South American Republics were established and the people of Paraguay became independent, they were unfit for self-government. Patriarchal rule carried to excess weakened the progressive power of the people, so that when deprived of their leaders and guides they were no longer able to struggle against the difficulties of their position [2].

Facts like these will furnish us with the necessary data for drawing a comparison between

[1] See his " Essay on the Influence of Authority in Matters of Opinion," 2nd edit., p. 192.

[2] " It was only after the influence of the Jesuits had emasculated the general mind of all sense of responsibility and every feeling of personal reliance that the whole race became the willing forgers of their own fetters."—Washburne's " History of Paraguay," i. p. 66.

the flourishing condition of Moravian settlements and the state of decay of similar institutions in Paraguay, which shall form the concluding portion of this chapter.

We saw in the previous chapter how, in the
case of the Moravian constitution, the direction
of affairs and the development of society was in
the hands of a representative and local self-
government. In the case of the Jesuit settlement, on the other hand, we have almost a
repetition, on a small scale, of the gradual development of the Church of Rome itself, which,
to use the words of M. Emile de Laveleye,
" consisting of a democratic republic at the
outset . . . . at the present time realises the
ideal of a theocracy, and of the most absolute
despotism imaginable." Social progress under
such rule is impossible, and hence we, find that
the Jesuits failed in raising the Indians pro-
gressively in the scale of society, whilst, as
we have seen, the Moravians, governing their
converts on the principles of civil and religious
liberty, produced a totally different result
among the natives of Greenland and Labrador.
This is the more noteworthy from the fact that
in these countries nature is much more sparing
in her gifts, and social advancement is rendered immeasurably more difficult from cli-
matic and constitutional obstacles, which only

well-sustained effort and frugal self-denial can overcome.

Again, while freedom encourages internal progress, its absence, even in the presence of comparative material equality, produces stagnation in social development. Whilst Bossuet was formulating the theory of Absolutism Milton was writing that of the Republic. And so, while the Modern Puritans, if we may so denominate the Moravians, have imported Anglo-Saxon free constitutions successfully into their growing settlements, the Jesuits have paid the penalty of following out Bossuet's maxim that rulers " are gods, and in a measure participate in the Divine independence," in the utter annihilation of their work in Paraguay.

While the Moravians have been careful from the first not to come into collision with the government in the countries of their dispersion, but have devoted themselves to carrying out the work of social regeneration by spreading the principles of Christianity, the Jesuits " pestered the court of Madrid with their intrigues, and embarrassed the local governments of America by their insubordination[1]," so as to

---

[1] " La Plata, the Argentine Confederation, and Paraguay," by Thomas J. Page, U.S.N., p. 499 *et seq.*

provoke a struggle between the temporal and spiritual power. This ended finally in their expulsion, in 1768, from the country, where, as in other Catholic countries, by reason of their conflicts with the civil power, the people became at last "a prey to internal struggles which consume their strength, or, at least, prevent them from advancing as steadily and rapidly as Protestant nations."

The progress of the Moravian settlements may thus be traced to their internal vigour and life, whilst the causes of the decrepitude of the Paraguay settlement must be sought in the deadening influences of artificial growth, the retarding tendencies of adherence to form, and a trust in force rather than in voluntary effort. If, then, we compare the habits of industry, frugal contentment, and advance of civilisation of the Moravian missions at the present day with the wretched and precarious condition of the surviving population in Paraguay, their rude manners and squalid poverty, their dogged apathy and servile demeanour, we cannot help being struck with the contrast. When, moreover, we compare the struggles and defeats of the Moravian society, maintaining itself through centuries, in spite of persecution, misfortunes, and even threatened extinction, with the promising beginnings and continued good fortune of the

Jesuit settlers in Paraguay, having all the advantages of superior knowledge, receiving augmented strength from papal and royal patrons, and meeting with scarcely any opposition from without, we cannot help being astonished at the respective results. In the one case, all but complete success and the promise of future improvement; in the other, a final and complete catastrophe, leaving no hope of recovery. We can scarcely help ascribing the result to the superior modes of government of the former over the latter, and the superiority of religious freedom in its influence on human affairs over ecclesiastical domination ; in fine, to the superiority of Protestantism encouraging self-expansion of the individual and the community over Romanism limiting the range of personal responsibility, and so laming the efforts of man in the aggregate, thus tending to social decline and national decay.

In tracing the historical evolution of the Moravian communities, and describing their present condition, we were unable to agree with those who profess to believe in the possibility of remodelling society after their pattern. If such was the unsatisfactory conclusion in the case of a society so far superior to the commonwealth of Paraguay, we need scarcely stop to point out the utter futility of viewing this latter experiment as a promising type of social architecture. It only serves as an interesting study of a peculiar phase of society, and as an example of a misguided, though well-intentioned, social experiment.

CHAPTER VII.

COMMUNISTIC SOCIETIES IN AMERICA. I.

IT was remarked by John Stuart Mill that "fair trial alone can test the workableness of any new scheme of social life." Now it so happens that many trials of this sort have been made, under favourable circumstances, on the rich virgin soil of America, by people thoroughly in earnest, in most cases possessing fair abilities and means as well as the spirit of self-denial required for such undertakings. Enthusiastic would-be regenerators of society have at various times left the Old Country for the Far West, prepared for almost any sacrifice in the attempt to found new communities on the basis of their respective theories.

Thus we meet with religious sects and social idealists full of faith in their own system, engaged in the very act of putting into practice in the New World Utopian experiments, the results of which are still before our eyes. We shall here describe these settlements, their foundation, development, and present condition, so as to measure the extent of their success. We shall compare the expectation with the fulfilment, and afford an opportunity to our readers to judge for themselves how far these Transatlantic settlements may or may not be regarded as models for the society of the future, and whether a further extension of their social system would be desirable in any attempts at the reconstruction of society.

In our examination of these social schemes, we shall note in each case the time and circumstances which favoured and gave the movement its chief impulse ; the nature, capacities, and resources of the emigrants themselves, from a mental, moral, and material point of view ; and the difficulties of their position in the new ground occupied by them. We shall also examine the constitution of each settlement, and consider whether the experience acquired thus far holds out any real hope of solving the labour-question by a more general adoption of like systems.

The main currents of emigration to the West that we purpose to consider owe their first impulse to the two movements which have exercised the greatest influence on European history —the Reformation and the French Revolution.

The social fictions of the sixteenth century, and the religious revivals of a later period, have their origin in the former movement; the Socialistic agitation of 1830, and the attempts at reform which followed, are closely connected with the latter.

The Shakers, Inspirationists, Harmonists, Oneida Perfectionists, and other bodies representing the class of religious Communists arose out of the Reformation movement; the secular division of American Socialisms, such as the Owenite settlements, Fourierist Phalanstères, and Icarian communes, was the fruit of the revolutionary movement of the last century. It will be seen in the sequel that those experiments have been most successful which have been inaugurated under religious auspices, while those lacking that element have only enjoyed an ephemeral existence.

In this work we shall consider only the religious Communists of America, beginning with an account of the *Shakers*, because, as we are told by a competent authority, their " influence on American Socialisms has been so great as to set them entirely apart from the other antique religious communities [1]." Their name is derived from the physical convulsions which shake their whole frame when under the

---

[1] Noyes, "History of American Socialisms," p. 595.

influence of strong religious fervour. They
themselves trace their origin, through the
French prophets of the last century, to the
Shakers of the Commonwealth [1]. But we find
no historical notice of them till about 1747,
when James Wardley, originally a Quaker, a
man of deep religious convictions, and under
the impression of having had supernatural
dreams and revelations, founded a small community, over which he and his wife Jane pre-
sided. Ann Lee, a blacksmith's daughter, of
Manchester, joined them in 1758. She appears
to have been a sincere religious enthusiast, by
no means devoid of practical sense. Humble-
minded, yet possessing natural dignity which
commanded confidence and respect, she became the head of the Shaker community in
America, by whom she was known as " Mother
Ann." She was only twenty-three years old
when she became a member of the society.
Twelve years later, when suffering persecution
with the sect to which she was attached, she
professed that, " by special manifestation of
Divine light, the present testimony of salvation and eternal life was fully revealed to her."

[1] Marsden, " Dictionary of Christian Churches and Sects,"
ii. 320–21. " The work," they said, " which God promised
to accomplish in the latter day, was eminently marked out
by the prophets to be a work of *shaking*." (Shaking the
heavens and the earth.)

Then she made the statement, on the ground of supernatural communication, that marriage was wrong, and "testified against it." Next " she was, by direct revelation, instructed to repair to America," where " the second Church would be established." Accordingly, Ann Lee embarked in May, 1774, at Liverpool for New York, accompanied by eight persons, mostly near relatives, including her husband, to whom she had been married long before her anti-matrimonial visions. It was by her exertions that for the time they maintained themselves in New York, and under her leadership they afterwards settled in " the woods of Watervliet, near Niskeyuna, about seven miles north-west from Albany." Having cleared the land, and after enduring endless hardships and vicissitudes, they received an accession of new adherents from the neighbouring Baptist community in New Lebanon, where a religious revival had led to the sudden exodus of those under its influence. In their wanderings they were attracted by the teachings and practice of self-denial of Ann Lee. They became her disciples, new converts were added in the immediate vicinity, and Mother Ann travelled from place to place to confirm these newly-planted churches in Massachusetts and Connecticut, having New Lebanon for their centre.

In 1805 there were twenty communities belonging to the Shakers. The population in 1847 was from 4,000 to 5,000. Since then there has been a decline in numbers, with a remarkable increase in prosperity.

When last visited by Mr. Charles Nordhoff (to whose interesting volume on "The Communistic Societies of the United States," published in 1875, we are deeply indebted in the present work) there were eighteen societies scattered over seven States, subdivided into fifty-eight "families," with an aggregate population of 2,415 souls [1], and owning real estate amounting to 100,000 acres.

These "families" form each a separate community of celibates of both sexes, of from thirty to ninety persons, who live together in one large house, a wide hall separating the dormitories of the men from those of the women. Buildings in which various industries are carried on by the brothers and sisters are grouped round this family mansion, for although agriculture forms the basis of their commonwealth, every member follows also some other avocation. They have a uniform style of dress, and in their social habits aim at extreme simplicity, while

[1] One of the branch communities, that at Tyringham, Mass., has lately been disbanded. Otherwise no marked changes have taken place since.

in practical life they are described as "industrious, peaceful, honest, highly ingenious, patient of toil. . . . They hold that he only is a true servant of God who lives a perfectly stainless and sinless life, and they add that to this perfection of life all their members ought to attain." They are pronounced Spiritualists, believing in the most intimate connection and communion with departed souls. Strange communications are received from the spirit-land at their religious meetings, instances of which are given by Mr. Noyes in his "American Socialisms [1]." Their religious services are peculiar. Mental prayers are preferred to audible petitions. Singing and dancing, "as David danced before the Lord," form the chief feature of their services. Marching round the assembly-room, at quick step, to a lively hymn-tune, the women following the men, all clapping their hands or holding them out to "gather a blessing," they work themselves into strong religious excitement, until one of the members, bowing before the elder or elders, suddenly begins a whirl, resembling that of the dancing dervishes of the East. Next they all solemnly kneel down in silent prayer, when some brother or sister is impressed to deliver

---

[1] Noyes, "History of American Socialisms," p. 605 *et seq.*

a message of comfort or warning sent from the spirit-land, or asks for the intercessory prayers of the assembly.

Evenings not spent in such religious exercises are devoted to family meetings, and innocent though by no means lively diversions, and instructive intercourse. On Sunday evenings they visit each other's rooms, three or four sisters visiting the brethren in each room by appointment, and engaging in singing and in conversation upon general subjects [1].

Their habits of life are frugal. They rise at half-past four in summer and five o'clock in winter; breakfast between six and seven, dine at twelve, and sup at six; by nine, or half-past, they are all in bed and lights are out. Each brother is assigned to a sister, who takes care of his clothing and linen, and has the oversight "over his habits and temporal needs." They eat in the general hall, and the preparation of food is left to the sisters, who take it in turn, as they also do the washing, ironing, and other light work.

Their diet is simple. All turn to work after breakfast, under the leadership of " caretakers," or foremen, who are subordinate to the deacons. But "Shakers do not toil

[1] Nordhoff, "Communistic Societies of the United States," p. 142.

severely ; they are not in haste to be rich. . . . Many hands make light work, *and where all are interested alike, they hold that labour may be made, and is made, a pleasure.*" There is no servant class, but, like the monks of old, they endeavour, as far as possible, to supply their own needs, without the use of outside labour. They are good and successful farmers, and their buildings are always of the best, whilst order and cleanliness are a distinctive feature of their settlements. As to external prosperity, Miss Harriet Martineau, after a visit to Mount Lebanon, is reported to have said : " A very moderate amount of labour has secured to them in perfection all the comforts of life that they know how to enjoy, and as much wealth as would command the intellectual luxuries of which they do not dream. The earth does not show more flourishing fields, gardens, and orchards than theirs. The houses are spacious, and in all respects unexceptionable. The finish of external things testifies to their wealth, both of material and leisure. If happiness lay in bread-and-butter and such things, these people have attained the *summum bonum.*"

In culture and the graces of life, the Shakers do not stand high. Although some of their members belonged formerly to the professional classes, while others have been mechanics, sea captains, and merchants, the bulk of the community are simple people. At the same time their successive leaders, from Ann Lee to Elder Frederick Evans, have been persons of shrewd character, and possessed of superior powers of management. The Shakers are not a reading people, and the libraries of their most cultured leaders are of extremely limited range. In the Shaker community at Canterbury they have, however, a fine school, with a special music-room. They take in twelve or fifteen newspapers, and have a library of 400 volumes, including history, voyages, travels, scientific works, and stories for children, but no novels. The society of Shirley is distinguished for its love of flowers, but we are told they do not cultivate any. The walls of the rooms are not adorned with pictures, but are lined instead with wooden pegs for hats, cloaks, and shawls, the useful being preferred to the ornamental. From this we may conclude that a taste for natural beauty, art, and literature is but imperfectly cultivated among the people. " It is an established principle of faith in the Church, that all who are received as members thereof do freely and voluntarily, of their own deliberate choice, dedicate, devote, and consecrate themselves, *with all they possess*, to the service of God for ever "—*i.e.* the Shakers accept *community of property* as their rule of life.   But results in this case, as in that of the Moravians, lead to the conclusion, that such a mode of life tends to hinder social progress and mental development. It keeps all on the same plane of rigid uniformity by means of rules and regulations, and prevents the expansion of the intellect into the regions of imagination and discovery.   Dulness and monotony characterise their daily life. The only recreation in this uninteresting existence is conversation among themselves, which, considering the paucity of subjects to be discussed, must become rather dreary at times.   In their more exciting religious entertainments are to be found, indeed, the merry sounds of song and dance, which, with the imaginary music from the land of spirits, produce a momentary exhilaration, but of a dreamlike, evanescent, imaginative character.   This however gives place immediately to the colourless sameness and sombre uniformity of every-day life.   " To a man or woman not thoroughly and earnestly in love with an ascetic life and deeply disgusted with the world," says Mr. Nordhoff, " Shakerism would be unendurable, and I believe insincerity to be rare among them.   It is not a comfortable place for hypocrites or pretenders."   We need not be astonished that the society is not fast increasing.   Since they cannot perpetuate themselves on account of their celibate life, and have also ceased to reinforce their ranks by the adoption of children, the rate of increase in membership has not kept pace with the vast accumulation of wealth, mainly in landed property. The society seems therefore in danger of painless extinction unless new religious revivals among other sects replenish their dwindling numbers[1].

The spirit of philanthropy accompanying the Methodist revival movement in England, which sought to elevate the masses of the people, and the expectations of the productive classes, excited by discoveries and improvements in machinery by Watt, Hargraves, Arkwright, and Crompton, were at their height when Ann Lee and her followers, impressed by this all-pervading spirit of social amelioration, determined to plant a new religious faith on the basis of a reformed society in America.

On the Continent a similar temper of the popular mind had produced a similar body of religious votaries, who, dissatisfied with what they called the deteriorated Christianity of the day, went to the United States to enjoy the free exercise of their particular opinions.

[1] For an interesting historical and descriptive account of the Shakers, see Mr. W. Hepworth Dixon's "New America," or the most recent work on "American Communities," by William Alfred Hinds, of Oneida, N.Y.

About the time when in this country Cowper in gentle accents sang of the common brother-hood of man, and Godwin advocated the rights of humanity in his " Caleb Williams," a man of the people, in Germany, without poetic genius or philosophical training, gave utterance in his own simple way to similar ideas, and determined to carry out practically these philanthropic aspirations. After deep thought and reflection, George Rapp, with 300 of his followers, set out for Baltimore on the 4th July, 1804, for the purpose of organising a new commonwealth in the Far West. Rapp was the son of humble parents, a man of slender attainments, but possessed independent thought, persevering industry, and the capacity for governing.

On landing he purchased 50,000 acres of wild land, and founded a Harmony Society in Pennsylvania. As most of his followers belonged to the peasant and mechanic class, he found in them the proper instruments for colonisation. They were thrifty, and few of them entirely destitute of means. It was agreed that they were to " throw all their possessions into a common fund, and to adopt a uniform and simple dress and style of house; to keep thenceforth *all things in common, and to labour for the common good of the whole body.*"

After some time, like the Shakers, they

adopted celibacy. The first beginnings of the
enterprise were on a humble scale. From forty
to fifty log-houses were erected, together with
a church, schoolroom, grist-mill, and some workshops. In the first two years 500 acres were
cleared, and other buildings and industries were
added. Ten years later they sold their land and
transferred their settlement to a more suitable site,
realising 100,000 dollars for the property. This
price was below the real value, which has been
estimated as at the least 150,000 dollars, which,
if divided among them, would have given 1,200
dollars to each head of a family, a considerable
sum if we consider that they began with probably
less than 500 dollars each family. So far the
Communistic experiment was a success. As
they increased in wealth they received large
accessions of emigrants from Germany. They
then agreed to burn their books, which stated
how much each had contributed, and determined henceforth to follow the maxim, "Mine
is thine." Their new settlement on the banks
of the Wabash, in Indiana, to which they had
removed, not proving so desirable a spot as
they had anticipated, they sold their estate of
Harmony to Robert Owen for 150,000 dollars,
and bought that of Economy, on the Ohio, near
Pittsburg, which they still occupy. Economy
is described as being "a model of a well-built,

well-arranged country village," and the Duke
of Saxe-Weimar Eisenach, who visited it in 1828,
speaks very favourably of the appointments in
the workshops and factories, of the healthy and
joyous appearance of the workmen and women,
as well as of the taste displayed everywhere
throughout the settlement.

In 1832 there was a secession of some members, owing to the intrigues of a scheming
adventurer, who called himself the Count of
Leon.   Fifteen thousand dollars were paid to
those members of the community who seceded
to become his adherents.   This shows a further
increase of capital during the twenty-seven
years of the society's existence.   The mystical
tendency of the members in their religious
seclusion, and their millenarian expectation
of a speedy advent of Christ, are in strange
contrast with their practical good sense and
thrifty habits of life.   They are not Spiritualists, like the Shakers, but Father Rapp
taught them to be practical Christians, and
inculcated the "duties of humility, simplicity of
living, self-sacrifice, love to neighbour, regular
and persevering industry, prayer and self-exami-
nation."   As they hold community of goods, in
imitation of the early Christians, to be one of
their articles of faith, every one is bound to
work with his own hands.   Their mode of daily

life resembles in most respects that of the Shakers. But their households consist of from four to eight men and women only, usually in equal numbers, and each family caters for itself. They are fond of flowers and music, painting and sculpture. Father Rapp's house contains a number of pictures of great value, and they have a library; still, the traveller was told, "the Bible is the chief book read among us."

Clothing is given out according to the requirements of each person, the tailor and the shoemaker each counting it a matter of honour or pride that the brethren shall be decently and comfortably clad.

"As each labours for all, and as the interest of one is the interest of all, there is no occasion for selfishness, and no room for waste. We were brought up to be economical; to waste is to sin. We live simply, and each has enough, all that he can eat and wear, and no man can do more than that." This was the explanation given to Mr. Nordhoff by a Harmonist in answer to some inquiries.

The relations of this society with the outer world, although at first it was viewed with suspicion and regarded with coldness, are most satisfactory in every respect. They are reported by their neighbours to be worth from two to three millions of dollars, which, in the eyes of the civilised world around them, no doubt, is an incontestable proof of their respectability. Moreover, we are told, the legal authorities of the United States, after a strict investigation, bear witness to the integrity and capacity of the rulers of the society in their management of an extensive and very complicated business, which is a remarkable testimony from unwilling witnesses in favour of the administrative power of the Communal system.

The present condition of the settlement is one of great external prosperity. Situated in one of the most picturesque spots near the Ohio river, the village of Economy and its surroundings produce a most favourable effect on the traveller's mind, whilst the placid, calm, and comfortable aspect of the inhabitants leaves no doubt as to their perfect contentment and peaceful happiness.

The smallness of the population may produce an unfavourable effect on the inquirer, since, owing to their celibate life, their numbers have dwindled down from 1000 in their best time to 100 at the present day, and most of these are aged. The young people, on reaching maturity, were allowed to decide between becoming full members of the society, or leaving it, or remaining as wages labourers. Many prefer the latter alternative, though in such

M

cases required to conform to the customs of the society, including celibacy. The greatest number prefer a life of complete independence to the restraints of communism, hence the rapidly diminishing numbers. There are indeed hired servants, but the hope of the future depends on twenty-five or thirty adopted children. Their large factories are closed, for there are no people to man them, and some of their other outlying works are carried on by means of Chinese labour and hired servants. But this does not trouble the Harmonists in the least. They expect the speedy appearance of Christ, and their chief aim is to prepare for it. In the meantime if asked what is to become of their vast property when they have passed away, their simple answer is, "The Lord will show us the way. We have not trusted Him in vain so far ; we trust Him still. He will give us a sign."

CHAPTER VIII.

COMMUNISTIC SOCIETIES IN AMERICA. II.

THE seceders from Rapp's colony at Economy, under the adventurer who called himself Count Leon, soon quarrelled with their leader, who ran away to Louisiana. Left thus without a head, they were glad to find a new leader in Dr. Keil [1], a mystic who, after passing

---

[1] Keil was a native of Prussia, and originally a man-milliner, but became a mystic and professed to cure diseases by means of magnetism. After living some time in New York he came to Pittsburg, and started as a physician, and showed, it is said, some knowledge of botany. He also professed to be the owner of a mysterious volume, written with human blood, and containing receipts for medicines, etc., that enabled him, as he professed, to cure various diseases. Presently he became a Methodist, and thereupon burnt this book with certain awe-inspiring formalities. He left the Methodists to form a sect of his own, and it is even related that he gave himself out as a being to be worshipped, and later, as one of the two witnesses in the Book of Revelation. In this capacity he gave public notice that on a certain day, after a fast of forty days, he would be slain in the presence of his followers. See Nordhoff, " Communistic Societies of the United States," p. 306. Mr. Nordhoff also conversed with him. After describing his personal appearance (p. 318), he says: " I thought I could perceive a fanatic, certainly a person of a very determined, imperious will, united to a narrow creed."

through various stages of religious fanaticism, gathered round him a small band of simple-minded Germans with the purpose of establishing a Communistic settlement like that of Rapp, without, however, adopting celibacy. Bethel, in Missouri, was chosen as their rallying-point, and soon the little community, possessed, indeed, of slender means, but of thrifty and energetic habits, began to grow in prosperity.

When Bethel had grown into a settled community, Keil, with the peculiar restlessness of his character, set out, accompanied by a few families, for Oregon, to found there, in the midst of the prairies, the new colony of Aurora. The Communists settled there possess at this moment 8000 acres of land, with lovely orchards and vineyards, saw-mills, tan-yards, and other industries, and are happy and contented after twenty years' trial of Communism. "Dutch Town," as the settlement is called by the Americans, is regarded as the paradise of Oregon, and the Aurora people are said to "have everything nice about them." The government is parental, and Dr. Keil is the ruling patriarch, with unlimited power. All members work for the common welfare, and draw the means of subsistence from the general treasury. But each family has its own house, or separate apartment, in one of the large buildings. Keil, who is their spiritual director as well as their economic guide, insists upon a community of goods as the corollary of the fundamental precept of Christianity, " Love one another."   " All selfish accumulation is wrong; contrary to God's law and natural laws."

Bethel in its main features resembles Aurora, and has a deputy-governor, appointed by Keil. Of both settlements it has been said, " that, considering what these people are, it cannot be denied that they lived better in community than they would have lived by individual effort."

Another body of religious enthusiasts from Germany, who called themselves the " True Inspirationists[1]," settled in 1842 near Buffalo, which they called Eben-Ezer.   The land here occupied proving insufficient for their purposes,

---

[1] This sect of Inspirationists is so called because of its belief in direct inspiration from heaven, and the " work of inspiration " is said to have begun far back in the eighteenth century.   In 1749, 1772, and 1776 there were special demonstrations.   In 1816 Michael Krausert, a tailor of Strasburg, became what they call " an instrument."   Others were added, and finally Barbara Heynemann, a " poor illiterate servant-maid," an Alsatian.   It was revealed to Christian Metz, who for many years was the spiritual head of the family, in 1842, that all the congregations should be gathered together, and led far away out of their own country, and America was pointed out as their future home.   Accordingly they went forth 350 strong at first, while others followed rapidly, until their number reached 1000, spread over different villages.

in 1855, "commanded by inspiration," they removed to their present home in Iowa, which they called by the Scriptural name Amana[1]. Originally they were not Communists, but declared that they adopted this mode of life because " we were commanded at this time, by inspiration, to put all our means together and live in community, and we soon saw that we could not have got on or kept together on any other plan."

This Amana community consists now of seven villages. The people live in separate houses, but have their meals in common.

Although professedly misogamists, warned by one of their teachers to " fly from intercourse with women, as a very highly dangerous magnet and magical fire," many of them follow the ordinary course of choice and courtship, which culminates in marriage, as is the case with other mortals not claiming to be inspired. Marriage, however, degrades them from a higher to a lower position in the commonwealth. The society numbers 1600 members, and owns 30,000 acres of land. It carries on agriculture and manufactures, and is in a highly prosperous condition. Street cars now run over the ground which thirty years ago was covered with a dense forest, and

[1] *Song of Solomon*, chap. 4, ver. 8.

fertile fields and gardens are spread over 30,000 acres cleared by the Inspirationists. It is " the largest and richest community in the United States," says Mr. Noyes. " The people of Amana appeared to me a remarkably quiet, industrious, and contented population ; honest, and of good repute among their neighbours ; very kindly ; and with religion so thoroughly and largely made a part of their lives, that they may be called a religious people," is the testimony of Mr. Nordhoff.

We shall not delay over the " Separatists " of Zoar, who, like the Rappists, belonged originally to Würtemberg, and, after many vicissitudes, settled in the midst of pathless prairies, which they succeeded in turning from a wilderness into a prosperous colony, and by systematic and associated labour and frugality acquired competence, if not affluence.

Having given some account of settlements owing their origin either to English or German enterprise, we come now to treat of a society which was originally formed by Americans, and consists mainly of American-born subjects—the " Perfectionists " of Oneida, and their branch society at Wallingford, in Connecticut.

The members of this society are descendants of New England Puritans, who, under the combined influence of religious revivals, and the Communistic theory which the Fourierist movement was spreading in America, formed themselves into a Perfectionist community, under the leadership of John Humphrey Noyes. Noyes, born in Brattleboro', Vermont, in 1811, was of respectable parentage and collegiate training. His adherents at first were few, and these, as in the case of Mohammed, members of his own household. But by degrees other communities in sympathy with him sprang up in the United States. His followers joined one of them, the "Brook Farm" community, founded by Unitarian Transcendentalists; "and thus, from a conjunction between the Revivalism of Orthodoxy and the Socialism of Unitarianism," was formed in 1848 the Oneida settlement in Madison County, New York. The amalgamated society acquired forty acres of land "on which stood an unpainted frame dwelling-house, an abandoned Indian hut, and an old Indian saw-mill. They owed for this property 2000 dollars. The place was neglected, without cultivation, and the people were so poor that for some time they had to sleep on the floor in the garret."

Still the followers of Noyes were not left without means, and in 1857 the members of all the associated communes had brought in the considerable sum of 107,706 dollars. They had to struggle against enormous difficulties, and to brave a hostile public opinion in the outside world. This they overcame by their energy and persevering efforts, and the remarkable excellence of their workmanship. Devoting themselves to agriculture and horticulture as their chief means of subsistence, they added various trades and manufactures in the course of time. In 1876 they had acquired 654 acres of land near Oneida, and 240 at Wallingford, which were laid out in orchards, vineyards, meadows, pasture and wood lands. The number of persons in both places amounted at the same time to 283. They also employ a large number of hired servants. Some of the members are lawyers, clergymen, merchants, physicians, teachers, but the majority are New England farmers and mechanics. They were moreover people of superior culture, to judge from the style and tone of the newspapers and other publications of the community, and from the first they have attached much importance to the influence of the Press. Mr. Hinds, the latest and most reliable authority on this head, being himself one of the Oneida Community, says, that the number has now reached 306, that they own 580 acres of good land in Oneida, and 366 acres in Wallingford [1].

[1] See his " American Communities," p. 120 et seq.

The name of this Community is derived from the religious dogma that total cessation from sin is closely connected with the institution of Communism and that human perfectibility and social regeneration go hand in hand. As the resurrection from the death of sin to the life of righteousness is not only a possible but a necessary condition of Perfectionism, so Communism is "the social state of the resurrection." They consider their own society, the Church on earth awaiting the approach of the Kingdom of God. Perfect holiness is the connecting link between the Church below and that above, and is the power by which the Kingdom of God is to be finally established in the world at large.

"Regeneration or salvation from sin, is the incipient state of the resurrection," we are told by Noyes. But we are rather shocked on discovering that among the signs of this incipient state of ultimate perfection are not only self-abnegation as to the rights of private property, but also the entire abrogation of the relationship between husband and wife. But like the Anabaptists, who taught similar doctrines, the Oneida Communists insist on self-denial and self-restraint, averring that "they must be Perfectionists before they are Communists." That stage having been reached, they affirm that there is "no intrinsic difference between property in person and property in things," and "complex marriage" used to be a necessary element in their reorganisation of society. But since 1879 this practice has been abandoned, and marriage and celibacy have become optional.

They still, however, have property in common, they eat at a common table, and have a common children's department. Thus, says an American writer to whom we are indebted for this information of recent date, the immoral and most objectionable features of their communities have been removed.

At Oneida the daily life is simple and steadily industrious, though not by any means laborious. "Mere drudgery they nowadays put upon their hired people." Their common dwelling-house is a large building, not without some architectural pretensions. It stands in the middle of a pleasant lawn, near the main road. The interior arrangements are good, and possess many modern improvements. On the second floor there is a large hall, used for the evening gatherings of the community, and furnished with a stage for musical and dramatic performances. On the ground floor is a parlour for visitors, and a library with files of newspapers and about 4000 volumes of books.

On each storey there are two large family rooms, and round them are situated the sleeping chambers. Above the dining-room is the printing office. Opposite this building, which has something of the characteristics of a Fourierist Phalanstère and an American hotel, are the offices, school-house, lecture-room, and chemical laboratory; farther on a carpenters' shop, a silk-dye house, and a small factory for the employment of children. There is also a large and conveniently-arranged laundry. The factories and workshops are situated at the distance of a mile; and a dwelling for thirty or forty of the Communists, having the oversight of the works, is erected on the spot. The Oneida farm is in excellent order, and the lawn before the main building, sheltered by plantations of ornamental trees, is a favourite resort for picnic parties coming from a distance.

The principle of administration is to do nothing without the general consent of the people. There are twenty-one standing committees on finance, and in addition to these, forty-eight departments for the general administration of the society's works. Women as well as men serve on committees. "Business boards" meet every week to discuss the secretary's report, and once a year there is a general meeting to consider the affairs of the society.

They do not despise accomplishments, but send some of their young women to New York to receive musical instruction, and their young men to the Scientific School, and other departments of Yale University, for their mental improvement. All cultivate vocal and instrumental music. The education committee superintend evening classes, and, together with the ordinary studies, teach French, Latin, and geology. The Perfectionists, so far from yielding to those stationary or retrogressive tendencies supposed to be inherent in Communistic bodies, have been the inventors of improvements in the manufacture of silk and various kinds of machinery, and have mastered difficult problems in their complicated enterprises, which prove them to be capable of industrial progress.

All members are subject to a system of mutual criticism, which tends to secure the good government of the community. Meetings are held every evening, which all are expected to attend, and thus opportunities are afforded for exhorting and administering reproof when necessary to members of the society. They have found this system work well, and assert that a "criticism cure" is almost as effectual as a "prayer cure." It has been suggested that mutual criticism serves mainly the purpose of counteracting the pride of mental pre-eminence and the consciousness of superior talent, which at all times is a standing danger to the carrying out of the principle of equality.

Fourier's suggestion of constant change in occupation is carried out, and the principle is even further extended, so as to avoid sameness and stereotyped habits in the community.

A committee is appointed which provides for the amusement of the Perfectionists, who may be seen disporting themselves in some secluded spot near the Oneida Lake, hunting, fishing, swimming, or rowing or skating like other people less perfect than themselves.

The society, having undergone many vicissitudes, and at length reached a high degree of prosperity, does not admit any new members to share the advantages acquired after years of struggle and self-denial. Here we have a resemblance to the more egotistical people of the outside world who decline sharing their hard-earned possessions with others. In this limitation they differ from the Primitive Christian Church, which they profess to follow. In fact it appears from this restriction in the carrying out of the Communistic idea, that even among the Perfectionists, who make Communism the chief article of their religious creed, the interest of self-preservation proves too strong for human nature, and that it is next to impossible to obliterate altogether the distinction between *meum* and *tuum*.

In concluding this branch of our subject, we cannot help suggesting a few reasons for the partial success of those settlements which have passed under review. Foremost among them is the power of religious enthusiasm, which at first binds such societies together into a common brotherhood, cemented by similar suffering and hopes, and maintained through all the changes and chances of life by a common belief, which separates the community from the rest of the world. They believe in a special providence governing their affairs, and therefore readily acquiesce in social regulations and restrictions for the common good, however irksome and unpalatable to the individual, because they are regarded as Divine appointments.

Again, but for periods of excitement, the additional members required to fill up gaps in the communities would not be forthcoming. Religious revivals (or movements so called), said Elder Frederick to Mr. Nordhoff, are " the hot-beds of Shakerism." "Our proper dependence for increase is in the Spirit of God working outside." So, on the other hand, the check on over-population by means of celibacy, or, as in the case of the Perfectionists, the "scientific" adjustment of population by State regulations to avoid economic embarrassment, becomes only possible in a society where self-discipline, passive endurance, and abstemious virtue, arising from strong convictions, can be relied upon.

Another cause of success is the sterling and almost brilliant capacity of most of the original leaders of those engaged in these Utopian experiments. Father Rapp in his dignified composure and unrivalled genius for organisation, and John Humphrey Noyes with his superior culture and keen perception of human character, are striking instances of this great power. On the other hand, where the leaders have been men of inferior capacity the progress of the society has been much less extensive, their present condition less prosperous, and their future prospect less encouraging. We have an instance of this failure in the Separatists at Zoar, founded by Joseph Bäumeler in 1816. "While he had strength," we are told by an eye-witness, Dr. Jacobi, "all went on seemingly very well; but as his strength began to fail, the whole concern went on slowly. I arrived the week after his death. The members looked like a flock of sheep who had lost their shepherd."

But what is still more important to notice is that most of the commercial successes of these settlements must be attributed to the fact that they are in a great measure trading communities in a new country where the demand generally exceeds the supply. They are therefore in constant communication with the outer capitalistic world, and so in fact owe their prosperity to the existence of a larger society resting on the old foundation, and are dependent on the egotistic principle of competition as a supplement to their own Socialism. Not only are all surplus commodities sold to these outsiders, but the drudgery work of the Communistic society is in most cases, now at least, performed by hirelings drawn from the same source, so that the social problems which make the introduction of Communism so difficult—namely: How the commercial risks of society may be forestalled and the lowest work of drudgery be provided for in a society of equals wanting the ordinary stimulus of exertion—have not as yet been solved by these Fraternities.

Moreover, the smallness of the scale on which the experiments have been made in these Utopian establishments leaves it an open question whether the same principles would be applicable to society at large. Montesquieu's opinion, that such

Commonwealths are scarcely practicable in larger States, is now an acknowledged truism, even among Communists themselves.

The great lesson, however, taught by the success of these social republics is the inestimable value of association labour, and the beneficial results arising from co-operative production.

CHAPTER IX.

"OLD MORTALITY OF SOCIALISM."

MANY years ago a sad-looking traveller made his appearance in one of the branch settlements of the Oneida community, to gain information about its constitution. He received from Mr. Noyes the soubriquet of "The Old Mortality of Socialism," because "he made it his melancholy business to wander from grave to grave, patiently deciphering the epitaphs of defunct Phalanxes." He was a Scotchman, of the name of Macdonald, and had been a follower of Owen in his early days. Made a wiser and a sadder man by experience, he resolved to write a work on Extinct Communisms. For this purpose he collected materials, which, in the form of a volume containing some 747 pages, fell into the hands of Mr. Noyes; but he died after having only written the Preface of his intended work. In it he explains his object. "At one time, sanguine in anticipating brilliant results from Communism, I imagined mankind better than they are, and that they would speedily practise those principles which I considered so true. But the experience of years is now upon me; I have mingled with 'the world,' seen *stern reality*, and now am anxious to do as much as in me lies to make known to the many thousands who look for a 'better state' than this on earth as well as in heaven, the amount of the labours which have been, and are now being, performed in this country to realise that 'better state.'" He determined to write a book " to waken dreamers, to guide lost wanderers, to convince sceptics, to re-assure the hopeful." He only succeeded, as we saw, in gathering valuable materials. These have been incorporated by Noyes[1], and as such form the basis of the present chapter. Some of our more sanguine readers will probably be impressed with melancholy feelings as was Macdonald when brought face to face with the facts of these Utopian experiments, and this sadness will be toned down to a still deeper hue as the results of these experiments are compared with the great expectations of those who engaged in them, when the ideals are contrasted with the realities, and the hopes with the

[1] See a full account in Noyes' "History of American Socialisms," pp. 1-10.

performances. But those who wish to have a complete and correct view, so as to form a well-balanced judgment on the subject, must follow us to the end in our inquiries into the nature of Utopias, theoretical and practical.

We shall now address ourselves to the Owenite and Fourierist schemes put into practice in America, together with some minor independent attempts. We shall in so doing present our readers with a short sketch of the latest efforts at social regeneration, before we bid adieu to Utopias, to give a brief account of more practical social experiments as exhibited in the co-operative movement.

We shall begin by a short account of the Owenite and kindred movements in America, which began in 1824, reached their height in 1826, and occupy altogether a short though eventful period in the history of Communistic experiments.

The followers of Rapp had prepared the way for Robert Owen, and it was from them, as we have seen, that he bought "New Harmony" in Indiana, as a home for his own community, which, however, differed radically from the earlier occupiers in the rigorous exclusion of every positive form of religion. The "industrious and well-disposed of all nations" were invited by Owen to New Harmony. In six weeks a population of 800 persons had been drawn together on the banks of the Wabash, and a few months later they numbered 1,000. It is allowed there were among them a good many " black sheep, . . . a proportion of needy and idle persons, who crowded in to avail themselves of Mr. Owen's liberal offer ; and . . . did their share of work more in the line of *destruction* than *construction*." The number and nature of the constitutions which succeeded one another with marvellous rapidity show the instability of the undertaking. The settlement begins as a " Preliminary Society," but is soon converted into a " Community of Equality," whilst the government passes from the hands of the executive council into Robert Owen's sole management. Presently this mode of imperialistic government leads to discontent and disintegration, and the community breaks up into several separate societies. Owen makes his celebrated declaration of mental independence, which abjures ancient ideas of private property, and marriage founded on it, and all " irrational systems of religion." The result is a new constitution, which abolishes all officers and provides for the election of three dictators to conduct the affairs of the society. Then a month later a new plan is proposed for the " Amelioration of the society, to improve the condition of the people, and make them more contented." Owen, with four joint-rulers, heads the movement. A sifting process takes place among the people. There is an appearance of order and increased happiness; but there is also with it a general tendency to return to the "old style," and people settle down here and there to follow their calling in the ordinary way. The principle of absolute Communism is abandoned, and "Individual Sovereignty" resumes its place. Great had been the expectations of Owen on starting the community. "Our principles," he said, "will, I trust, spread from community to community, from state to state, from continent to continent, until this system and these *truths* shall overshadow the whole earth, shedding fragrance and abundance, intelligence and happiness, upon all the sons of men." But how different the result! Three years after its establishment we hear of the general break-up of the New Harmony, which had become a new discord, and similar was the fate of other like societies, founded as they all had been on a total misapprehension of human nature.

The disinterested industry, and the absence of selfishness in the acquirement of exclusive property, of which Owen had dreamed, were not to be found among the thousand democrats whom he had collected around him, and whom no religious bond held together. They had taken possession of the 30,000 acres of land and the ready-made village bought from the Rappists, but being little better than a rough set of adventurers, they possessed none of the virtues of endurance, energy, and frugal self-devotion, which are required to make a social scheme of this kind even moderately successful. The absence of unanimity of counsel among such a heterogeneous body, and the unwillingness to obey constituted authorities, speedily gave the deathblow to the Utopian experiment.

The following extract, describing the gradual decline of the Yellow Springs Community, one of the more promising of the eleven settlements founded by Owen, in Indiana and New York, in Ohio, Tennessee, and Pennsylvania, may serve as a type of the fate of all: " For the first few weeks all entered into the new system with a will. Service was the order of the day. Men who seldom or never before laboured with their hands devoted themselves to agriculture and the mechanic arts with a zeal which was at least commendable, though not always according to knowledge. Ministers of the gospel guided the plough, called the swine to their corn, instead of sinners to repentance, and let patience have her perfect work over an unruly yoke of oxen. Merchants exchanged the yard-stick for the rake or pitchfork. All appeared to labour cheerfully for the common weal. Among women there was even more apparent self-sacrifice. Ladies, who had seldom seen the inside of their own kitchens, went into that of the common eating-house, and made themselves useful among pots and kettles; and refined young ladies, who had all their lives been waited upon, took their turn in waiting upon others at the table. And several times a week all parties who chose mingled in the social dance in the great dining-hall.

" But notwithstanding the apparent heartiness and cordiality of this auspicious opening, it was in the social atmosphere of the community that the first cloud arose. Self-love was a spirit which could not be exorcised. It whispered to the lowly maidens, whose former position in society had cultivated the spirit of meekness, ' You are as good as the formerly rich and fortunate ; insist upon your equality.' It reminded the favourites of former society of their lost superiority, and, in spite of all rules, tinctured their words and actions with the love of self. Similar thoughts and feelings soon arose among the men. . . . It is unnecessary to descend to details ; suffice it to say that at the end of three months—*three months !*—the leading minds in

the community were compelled to acknowledge
to each other that the social life of the community could not be bounded by a single circle.
They therefore acquiesced, but reluctantly, in
its division into many little circles. Still they
hoped, and many of them no doubt believed,
that though social equality was a failure, community of property was not. But whether the
law of *mine and thine* is natural or incidental in
human character, it soon began to develop its
sway. The industrious, the skilful, and the
strong saw the products of their labour enjoyed by
the indolent, the unskilled, and the improvident,
and self-love rose against benevolence. . . . For
a while, of course, these jealousies were only
felt, but they soon began to be spoken also. It
was useless to remind all parties that the common labour of all ministered to the prosperity
of the community. *Individual* happiness was
the law of nature, and it could not be obliterated ;
and before a single year had passed this law had
scattered the members of that society, which
had come together so earnestly and under such
favourable circumstances, back into the selfish
world from which they came.

" . . . They admitted the favourable circumstances which surrounded its commencement,
the intelligence, devotion, and earnestness which
were brought to the cause by its projectors, and

its final, total failure. And they rested ever after in the belief that man, though disposed to philanthropy, is essentially selfish, and that a community of social equality and common property is impossible."

Ex uno omnes disce. Well begun—sadly ended, is the epitaph for every one of the Owenite settlements in North America.

Massachusetts has been called " the great mother of notions," and among the large progeny of " isms " to which she gave birth was Socialism. Several Communistic experiments took rise on her soil. Of Brook Farm we shall have occasion to speak farther on, but one or two experiments anticipatory of Fourierism we must mention in this place.

Hopedale was founded by the Rev. Adin Ballow, and owed its origin to the religious impulse of Universalism. It was designed to be a " miniature Christian Republic," and its object was to harmonise individual freedom with social co-operation. It was intended to expand into a grand confederation of similar communities, " a world ultimately regenerated and Edenised." Mr. Ballow was first President, but was superseded by a more business-like organiser, E. A. Draper, who managed, by degrees, to buy up three-fourths of the joint-stock, and obtain legal control over the property. Things went on unsatisfactorily; loans were incurred, and capital sunk in unprofitable enterprise. Draper paid the debts of the society, and, we presume, became owner of the property. The Hopedale experiment terminated in a failure. Another and similar Yankee attempt and forerunner of Fourierism was the North Hampton Association. It was established with the usual flourish of trumpets by a small but enlightened set of religious Universalists. Labour was to be remunerated equally, both sexes and all occupations receiving the same compensation. A common family and a common table were instituted for those who preferred it. A " Preamble and Articles of Association" was adopted in 1843, tending towards consolidation and Communism, and a department of education was organised, in which it was designed to unite study with labour, so as to encourage both physical and mental development. In the course of the third year, people interested in the subject of social reform were solicited to subscribe to a loan of 25,000 dols., to support the society in its struggles. This appeal was not responded to, and pecuniary difficulties arose which produced disunion and distrust, aggravated by religious dissensions, which hastened the downfall of the community.

The excitement produced by the anti-slavery

movement came to its climax in 1843, and
served as a powerful feeder of the Socialistic
fervour which the writings of Fourier, as in-
terpreted by Albert Brisbane, were producing
in the United States. John A. Collins, an
active Abolitionist, became the founder of the
Skaneatales Community. Avoiding some of
the dangers which had proved fatal to similar
schemes, the organisers of this movement took
care not to introduce the "gaseous class of
mind," and looked out for men of "stability of
character, industrious habits, physical energy,
moral strength, mental force, and benevolent
feelings," as indispensable characteristics of
the "valuable Communist." They recognised
that at first there should be as few non-pro-
ducers as possible, single men and women and
small families, and accordingly the experiment
did not fail through pecuniary embarrassment.
On the contrary, when the community had
reached the third year of its foundation the
value of its property had been doubled. Nevertheless it was dissolved, partly because its two
chief leaders could not agree, and partly because
the freedom and enjoyment of home-life was
constantly spoiled by the over-virtuous desire
of every member to be an example of abstemi-
ousness to his neighbour. A community where
everybody, by precept and example, wished to

prevail on everybody else to adopt his own mode of life as the best, became most uncomfortable, and, as we might expect, in less than three years it was dissolved.

These settlements were, so to speak, the prelude to the introduction of the Fourierist Phalanx. The latter had their own independent theory of social architecture, but obeyed the common impulse to social reform, produced by the spread of Fourier literature, aided by the religious and political excitement of the period.

The "New York Tribune" opened its columns to the propounders of Fourierist theories. Horace Greeley, its chief editor, became a warm supporter of the Socialist propaganda. From March, 1842, to May, 1843, Brisbane was engaged in beating the drum, and the consequence was that in the summer of 1843 "Phalanxes by the dozen were on the march for the new world of wealth and harmony." Western New York responded most vigorously to the call, and great successes were reported from what has been called the "Volcanic District." A practical attempt was made to organise a *confederation* of associations. A league was formed, called the "American Industrial Union," and several Phalanxes were established on Fourierist principles.

The first of these was the Sylvania Association. There was no lack of enthusiasm at its start, nor want of talent in the promotion of its interests. Warm friends of the cause in New York and Albany procured a favourable site in Pennsylvania, with 23,000 acres of arable land. Temporary buildings were erected for the 150 settlers who took possession, and who appeared contented and happy in their new domain, and gratified with the novel modes of life. But jealousies crept in, discipline was disregarded, the working community was found to be deficient in intelligence, idleness and greediness told unfavourably on the resources of the association, and all engaged in it incurred loss. The capital expended on the experiment was estimated at 14,000 dollars ; the result obtained, *nil.* A speedy dissolution followed.

A similar story might be told of a good many other associations of the same kind, all ending in general disappointment, the causes assigned being the acquisition of unfavourable sites or the insufficient training for such experiments of those engaged in them, and more often the want of harmony among the members. To give a short history of them would occupy more room than we could afford, and would only weary the reader by endless repetition. We shall conclude our account of North American experiments with a comparative view of the famous trio of Fourierist associations, the Wisconsin Phalanx, the North American Phalanx, and Brook Farm.

The first of these was founded by the zeal of many leading citizens of Racine County. It was unburdened with debt, and its organisation into groups and series, as recommended in Fourier's system, appears to have worked admirably at first. Only persons of good character, physique, and income were admitted to the association; and the principles of Christianity were recognised as the best means for elevating individual character, and harmonising society. The development of mind by the refining process of education was attended to with care, and for a time the industrial association prospered, so much so that at the division of property when it was finally dissolved a premium was paid ·on its stock, instead of a loss being incurred as in other similar experiments. What then was the cause of its dissolution?

Selfishness it was feared from the first would become the principal object of progress; and so it proved in the end. Many members had accumulated private property; the prosperous condition of the society, as in the case of some friendly societies in the present day, led to a general desire to divide the profits. Differences of opinion as to the future policy of the community furnished another pretext for a speedy dissolution, and so the experiment was abandoned because "its leading minds became satisfied that under existing circumstances no important progress could be made, rather than from a want of faith in the ultimate practicability of association." It was a deliberate suicide. The attempt had been highly successful from a pecuniary point of view. Its success became the cause of its failure as a society.

A still more successful undertaking was the North American. It was the test-experiment, as its proud name implies. Horace Greeley was Vice-president of the society, which being situated near New York, and under excellent management, was intended to be the model Phalanx, and did actually surpass the rest in success and longevity. Literature and the press had paved the way. Persons of importance, impressed by the sublime promises of Fourier and the vista of potentialities in social improvement held out by his interpreters, formed themselves into a body under the name of "The Albany Branch of the North American Phalanx," and began the work of the association with an aggregate subscription capital of 8000 dollars. The framing of the constitution caused, at first, much labour and anxiety. A controversy arose whether it was

o

to be a joint-stock co-operative association, or a Phalansterian or serial organisation. The latter form was finally adopted. A graduated hierarchy of orders was appointed for the purposes of administration, although the principle of personal liberty was recognised as indispensable for the purpose of encouraging individual development. In fact, the progressive development of man and society was one of the chief articles of belief of the association. The establishment of true social relations, and harmonious association to enable the labourer to acquire the means of comfort, education, and refinement, together with a distribution of property on the basis of religious justice, were the objects sought to be attained.

For these purposes the association was started with the capital subscribed by the promoters. Its entire population in 1844 consisted of seventy-seven persons, including women and children. Eight years later it had risen to 112, and its property was estimated at 80,000 dollars, *i.e.*, ten times the amount originally subscribed.

No wonder that the review of their success inspired the promoters with pride and confidence. They claimed to have paved the way for the final unification of society, by practically carrying into effect Fourier's formula, "Equit-

able distribution of profits." They claimed to
have fairly "closed the first cycle of our so-
cietary life efforts," and to have "laid the germ
of living institutions, of the co-operations which
have perpetual life . . . which only need a
healthy development to change without injustice, to absorb without violence, the discords of
existing society, and to unfold, as naturally as
the chrysalis unfolds, into a form of beauty, a
new and higher order of human society."

All they required to extend the work so fairly
begun was larger means, and additional numbers of people *who were willing to work for an
idea.*

A picture is drawn of the "enchanting do-
mains" of this interesting society in 1845, when
it was visited by some of its New York patrons,
which satisfies all doubts as to the unsurpassed
prosperity and capacity for refined enjoyment of
the members of the Phalanx. But for all that
there was a skeleton in the cupboard; for too
soon want of sufficient working capital hampered
progressive development; grumbling was heard
among the members in consequence of the insufficient reward of labour. This wages question,
if we may so call the dispute, led to the secession
of some, who formed a society of their own,
less Communistic in its tendencies. Religious
dissensions, occasioned or fomented by emis-

saries from without, also tended to undermine the harmonious well-being of the society. People who would work for an idea could not be found in sufficient numbers to develop the resources of the land. The character of those already located in the settlement had begun to deteriorate, culture and education were neglected, the desire for animal gratification increased in proportion, the society got heavily into debt, a destructive fire consumed a considerable portion of its property and hastened on its dissolution. " Each for himself," became the common cry, and after the experiment had been tried for little more than twelve years, promising above measure though it had been at one time, like all other communistic movements it came to an inglorious end.

Hawthorne, Dr. Channing, and Theodore Parker are mentioned by Emerson[1] as the most distinguished members of that small literary band of socialistic transcendentalists who, after the manner of Ruskin's Society of St. George, engaged in a tentative system of social regeneration in the parcel of land called " Brook Farm." They established a sort of joint-stock community, which afterwards was converted into a Fourierist Association. Some of the social idealists, like Hawthorne, who first took an

[1] "Reminiscences of Brook Farm."

interest in it, after a time abandoned the enterprise as impractical. Others, carried away by the Fourierist enthusiasm of the time, helped to turn it into a Phalanx, according to the law of groups and series, as the basis of the new industrial organisation. The society was divided into three primary departments of labour—agricultural, domestic, and mechanical —and great expectations were entertained as to its future success.

At the National Convention of Associationists, which assembled at Clinton Hall, New York, on April 4th, 1844, the prospects of the principle of association were compared to the tokens of approaching land which cheered the drooping spirits of Columbus and his companions. The friends from Brook Farm were the birds, and those from other settlements the flowers that floated on the waves. A representative from Brook Farm, Mr. Dana, spoke of the favourable results, after a few years' trial there, of the association principle, such as the abolition of domestic servitude, and the raising of manual labour to "its just rank and dignity in the scale of human occupations." Referring to the relations between capital and labour outside, and comparing them with the just distribution of work and wages in Brook Farm, the speaker went on to say:—

"We have established a true relation between

labour and the people, whereby the labour is done not entirely for the benefit of the capitalist, as it is in civilised society, but for the mutual benefit of the labourer and the capitalist. We are able to distribute the results and advantages which accrue from labour in a joint ratio.

"These, then, very briefly and imperfectly stated, are the practical, actual results attained. In the first place, we have abolished domestic servitude; in the second place, we have secured thorough education for all; and in the third place, we have established justice to the labourer and ennobled industry. . . . We have by actual facts, by practical demonstration, proven this, viz., that harmonious relations, relations of love, and not of selfishness and mutual conflict, relations of truth, and not of falsehood, relations of justice, and not of injustice, are possible between man and man."

It was hoped that Brook Farm would form the nucleus of fraternal co-operation throughout North America, which would thence spread far and wide, so as to bring about "the final establishment of happiness and peace among the nations of the earth."

The "Brook Farm Association for Education and Industry" changed its name in 1845, and became the "Brook Farm Phalanx," starting with a new constitution. It served as the virtual centre of the Fourierist propaganda, and became the head-quarters of the American Union of Associationists, having for its motto—

"Unity of man with man in true society;

"Unity of man with God in true religion;

"Unity of man with nature in creative art and industry."

The programme published on this occasion concludes thus: "We are sure to conquer. God will work with us; humanity will welcome our work of glad tidings. The future is ours. On! in the name of the Lord."

Emissaries were sent forth to establish affiliated societies. Meetings were held to persuade the public. The "Harbinger," the organ of the new society, became a vigorous exponent of its views; but within a year from the time when it commenced this task of propagating Fourierism, a disastrous fire prostrated the energies and hopes of the association. Still, there was as yet no interruption of the internal harmony, and the "Harbinger" spoke cheerfully of the brotherly love and devotion to the cause prevailing among the members. Soon, however, signs of rapid decay set in, and the society, and with it all hopes of the success of Fourierism in America, came to an end. "The gift of tongues" among its original promoters, added to their spiritualistic tendency, which began in religious transcendentalism, and ended in Swedenborgianism, together with the verbal controversies and impractical sentimentalism which arose, are said to have been the chief reasons of this most conspicuous failure in the latest form of Utopian experiment.

There are other minor associations, such as the Brocton Community, near Lake Erie, combining Spiritualism and Socialism, which our limited space prevents us from describing. The result in all these cases is the same. After a flourish of trumpets and a few years' trial they came to a speedy end. "It crowed cheerily in its time," says the historian of American Socialisms of one of them. The epitaph of another runs like this, and is applicable to all: "It effected but little, and was of brief duration. No further particulars." It is the same story throughout slightly diversified. Lack of faith in the experiment, want of funds, disharmony and distrust, quarrels over title-deeds, suspicion of the "money-bags[1]," indolence, and ignorance as to the principles of association, bad selection of the soil, the self-seeking of the managers frequently neglecting or disregarding the interests of the association, the standing danger of returning to the "flesh-pots of Egypt" (*i.e.* the ordinary modes of industry after the accumu-

[1] i. e. the contributions of capital.

lation of property and profit), faulty distribution and unforeseen disasters—these are some of the causes of failure and the inherent disintegrating infirmities of such societies[1].

If such be the end of the associations in North America, with its wealth of territory and great popular enlightenment, with its favourable constitution, encouraging the spirit of free association according to the national motto, " *E pluribus unum*," what may be expected of similar experiments in the Old World, with its land-famines, its over-population, and the many corrupting social influences which have not yet

[1] Besides the communities here described, and selected on account of their long-established fame, there are a few others which have since struggled into existence, such for example as "The Brotherhood of the New Life," a social experiment tried at Salem-on-Erie, in which Mr. Laurence Oliphant once took a great interest, and a full description of which may be found in Mr. Hinds' book, p. 140; and the "Adonai-Shom" community, which has existed in Athol, Massachusetts, for the last sixteen years, consisting of twelve members and owning 210 acres of land. Several co-operative industrial associations also have been started with or without communal homes, such as the city of Greeley, Colorado, with a population of 4000, and the "Prairie Home" in Franklin County, Kansas, founded by E. V. Bossière, a French gentleman of wealth and culture, on Fourierist principles. All these are in existence and wait their trial, but Mr. Hinds "regards them one and all as additional evidences that a tidal wave of Socialism—using this term in its broadest sense—is bearing society onward toward conditions more accordant with its ultimate destiny."

taken root on the other side of the Atlantic? If all attempts to reorganise society on a new basis failed even when supported by so much religious and moral enthusiasm, are we not entitled to say that the logic of facts has pronounced an unfavourable verdict on such Utopian experiments?

It has been said that Fourier's system never had a fair chance in America, that his apostles and followers did not understand fully or carry out faithfully his principles, and that, therefore, he is not responsible for their failure. It seems to us that this is not so. We think that his theories did receive a fair trial, and that their failure is unfavourable to Fourier's hypothesis as to the forces and capabilities of human nature, and the forms of life and society founded on it. Proceeding inductively, with the foregoing facts before us, we must come to the conclusion that whilst the principle of association itself deserves our most anxious consideration in speculating on any possible improved system of society, its practical application by Owen, Fourier, Cabet, and their followers has proved a decided failure. These social philosophers in fact prematurely anticipated the moral and social development of humanity, led away by hasty and erroneous generalisations in social science.

CHAPTER X.

SOCIAL PALACES.

WE have now done with Utopias, and shall proceed to the consideration of more practical social experiments — co-operation at home and abroad. We have given some account of communistic schemes founded on religious enthusiasm in the early period of the Christian Church; among the monastic orders and the Pre-reformation mystics, among the native converts under Jesuit rule in South America, among Protestant Separatists seeking religious and civil liberty in the United States, among sober-minded Unitarians, among philosophical Universalists, and among anti-religious Secularists. We have seen how all founders of Utopias resemble each other in having great expectations which are mostly doomed to end in disappointment, in starting with a promising beginning which almost invariably culminates in complete failure.

In the most recent of these experiments,

when the "new science of associated industry," as taught by Fourier, was applied under very favourable circumstances for the construction of his "new social edifice of matchless and indescribable beauty, and true architectural symmetry," as an American orator enthusiastically called it, the final result was most discouraging. We have seen how the Brook Farm association after a few years of success ended in talk, and yet it was the most perfect of these attempts. Its promoters declared that "productive labour, art, science, and the social and religious affections, will be wisely and beautifully blended and combined, and they will lend reciprocal strength, support, elevation, and refinement to each other, and secure abundance, give health to the body, development and expansion to the mind, and exaltation to the soul."

If asked what is the cause of the failure of these Utopian experiments, we shall have little hesitation in replying that it is due to the introduction of social constitutions before men's minds were ripe for them; to an unwarrantable trust in revolution instead of a cautious advance in the direction of social reformation; to the disregard of that great truth taught by all history, that human character and human institutions have been slowly developed and adapted to existing circumstances in the course of ages ; and that constitutions, social as well as political, to be lasting must be allowed to grow slowly, and cannot be called into existence ready-made at the command of social idealists.

The truth of the principle of association which lies at the foundation of all these schemes of social amelioration cannot be denied ; in fact, it is as old as humanity itself. Its practical failure is to be explained by its misapplication with respect to time, place, and external surroundings. Society began in Communism, as M. de Laveleye, in his great work on "Primitive Property," has abundantly shown, just as there exists a sort of Communism in every family where all work for each and each for all—in fact it is the primitive order of society. But as families grew into tribes, and tribes into nations by confederation and conquest, the ruling few, whether they derived their power from physical or mental superiority, soon subjected the many to slavery, and then we find the work done by the many for the few, as in the states of antiquity, and in a modified form in the feudal ages. The French Revolution marked the partial victory of the principle of equality, after more than a thousand years' struggle against this forced labour in human societies. We say partial victory, because, whilst securing the individual liberty and equality of all in the eyes of the law, the French Revolution helped little to promote material equality. For, during the competitive struggle which followed the liberation of the masses from the tyranny of the old *régime*, the few favoured by nature and fortune, intellect and money, prevailed over the many, who lacked these advantages. This led to the despotism of capital, as Socialists call it. Two further revolutions were attempted to bring about another emancipation from the thraldom of competition, having for their object the promotion of social equality, and the re-establishment of the principle of fraternity in a world where class interests and class conflicts had set every man against his brother. The tendency of society no doubt is now in the direction of equality and fraternity, towards a communion of interest between man and his fellow, and, by means of free combination and co-operation, to effect the ultimate solidarity of the human race. This is a natural historical sequence following upon historical precedents. But to hasten on the process artificially, or by violent change, only retards the progress of society. The over restless spirit of social reformers, as well as the lethargic indifference to improvement, and the stupid antagonism to change which mark their opponents, are alike reprehensible and destructive.

The true method of the social reformer is to wait for opportunities, to watch the signs of the times, and to adapt himself to the varying circumstances of the hour, to bring about by slow degrees improvements in the economic condition of the toilers of mankind, and a more equitable distribution of work and enjoyment in the world at large.

The general adoption of the principles of co-operation in the production as well as in the distribution of commodities, in work as well as in the enjoyment of the wealth produced by it, promises to do for humanity what the adoption of Communism has failed to accomplish. As one of the Socialistic pioneers has told us :—

"Great changes require a slow movement. All pioneers should remember to be constructive, and not merely destructive—not to tear down faster than they can substitute something better."

"Every failure of association which has come to my knowledge," he declares as the result of his own experience, "has been in consequence of disregarding these conditions ... they have attempted too much. Having, in most cases, torn down the isolated house-hold and family altar (or table) before they had even science enough to draft a plan of a

Phalanstery, or describe a unitary household, they seemed in some cases to imagine that the true social science, when once discovered, would furnish them, like the lamp of Aladdin, with all things wished for. They have awakened from their dreams, and now is the time for practical attempts, to start with, first, the joint-stock property, the large farm or township, the common home and joint property of all the members; second, co-operative labour and the equitable distribution of products . . . third, educational organisation . . . fourth, the Phalansterian order, unitary living. As this is the greatest step, it requires the most time, most capital, and most mental preparation. . . . In most cases many years will be required for the adoption of the second of the conditions, and more for the third, and still more for the fourth . . ." etc., etc.[1]

Without committing ourselves to this doctrine of Social Evolution ending in the Phalanstery, we may at all events accept the writer's experience in favour of the slow changes to be expected in the process of social amelioration. We must also agree with him in the importance he attaches to the co-operative system which now promises such great results. The

[1] From a letter of Warren Chase, the founder and principal manager of the Wisconsin Phalanx. See "American Socialisms," p. 432.

increase in the number of joint-stock companies, the use made of distributive stores, the establishment of numerous co-operative societies, both at home and abroad, all show the advancing tendency of society. It is well known that stability of character, industrious habits, physical courage, moral strength, mental vigour, benevolent feelings, and the power of self-denial and devotion to the public good, are indispensable to any society founded on the principle of common interest as opposed to individual egotism or self-interest. Any society founded on rigidly applied principles of equality cannot exist without those qualities. Their absence has almost invariably proved the stumbling-block, as we have seen, to most of the Communistic societies described. Such qualities must therefore be acquired and fostered as a preliminary to the success of any general scheme of social equality. Now co-operation helps in thus forming character, and paves the way gradually, by construction and not destruction, to a more equitable distribution of wealth. We have seen that, in spite of ignorance and mistakes, imperfections and despotism, the weakest of these Communistic societies, in adopting the co-operative principle, financially succeeded for a time—that even when they failed, in their last gasp they pronounced it to be the true Catholicon for existing

P

social evils. With the application of this principle all went on well as long as the enthusiasm in the rank and file of the community lasted, and the right men were able to retain the lead, and before partial failure and the introduction of discordant and weak elements produced lukewarmness and discontent.   Even after organic disease, followed by decay and death, had set in, there was regret in the final abandonment of the associative principle, as was the case when the North American Phalanx was dissolved. Still, under the most desponding circumstances, those engaged in the experiment exclaimed with Meeker : "Men are generally not prepared. *Association is for the future.*" This is an encouragement to the believers in the associative principle ; it is also a warning against hazardous experiment with insufficient means, or insufficiently developed forces in those who lead or those who follow in the movement. Co-operation promises to provide those necessary securities, and to form a safe bridge for the progress of society from the present forms of individualism to a more satisfactory state of federal union.

In order to test the true value of co-operation we shall now consider some instances where the principle has been practically attempted.

The different kinds of co-operation may be roughly divided into three classes, viz., 1. Humanitarian co-operation, which is patronising in its main features, and has its origin in the philanthropy of capitalists and others ; 2. Patriarchal co-partnership, founded on the principle of mutual interests, which allows the working men to share in the profits of the employers, whilst the latter still retain the chief management of the business. 3. Fraternal co-operation, which is co-operation proper, *i.e.* the combination among the working men themselves to establish concerns for which they are solely responsible, becoming thus their own employers, and combining the character of master and men in their own persons. These orders of co-operative enterprise mark the successive steps from capitalistic modes of industry to association labour, which, some think, will probably become generally prevalent in the society of the future.

Most persons have heard of Boucicaut's enormous general store in Paris, the "Au bon marché," which carries on twenty-four different branches of trade on the same premises, having under its employ no less than 2000 persons, of whom 1400 or 1500 reside on the premises, while all are provided with board. There are four dining saloons, in which 250 assistants can take their meals at the same time. They breakfast in turns between nine and eleven o'clock in the morning, and dine between six and seven in the evening. There is a special refectory for the ladies of the establishment, and another for the remainder of the employés. Saloons and billiard-tables are provided by the employer for the amusement of the young men in the evening, and instruction is given in music, languages, and fencing, as well as lectures on history and other subjects by the best professors. There is a ladies' saloon where similar opportunities for self-improvement in literature and art are offered to the female section of the establishment.

All more or less participate in the profits of the concern, and the shares rise in proportion to the position attained in the various grades of employment. As all are directly interested, there is a general desire to please customers, and so increase the extent and enhance the profits of the business. Every one of the twenty-four " chefs," or heads of departments, are trusted and experienced men, and meet for consultation in urgent cases. The complex organisation of so extensive a business requires a whole regiment of trustworthy cashiers, bookkeepers, secretaries, and others, who perform their task conscientiously and to the best of their ability, as their own personal interest is more or less linked' to the prosperity of the firm. Here then, we have an example of a practical as well as humanitarian effort at co-operation, which has all the advantages of a Communistic Society with hardly any of its risks and drawbacks. The success of the undertaking is proved by the fact that M. Boucicaut, who is described as an entirely "self-made" man, left several millions of property on his death in 1877. Since 1879 his widow conducts the business with a working capital of 20,000,000 francs, on the same principles as her husband. The reserve fund, created in 1876 and augmented by yearly contributions set apart by the firm out of the profits for the benefit of those who do not otherwise participate in the profits, has steadily risen to the handsome sum of 567,843 francs. It is intended to provide payments of sums of money, according to length of service and in proportion to wages received, to the family or representative of any one who may die in the employ, or who may be incapacitated by old age or other causes. Each person has thus a sort of private account which amounts to a provision against sickness and old age, and a life insurance in case of death. There are now 592 such persons apart from those who have a direct interest in the profits of the firm. A similar plan on a smaller scale has been adopted by Messrs. Cassell, Petter, and Galpin, La Belle Sauvage Yard, London.

The "Women's Hotel" in New York, which

covers 20,000 square feet of ground, and is seven storeys high, containing 502 private apartments, a dining-room for 600 guests, and a kitchen fitted to provide for 5,000 persons, was erected from purely humanitarian motives by the well-known millionaire, A. T. Stewart, to afford a comfortable abode for about a thousand young women of good character who have no homes of their own in the great city. The hotel combined the solidity, elegance, and comfort of private houses of the best class. It contained a suite of handsomely - furnished reception-rooms, and a library of 2,500 volumes. Enclosed by the four blocks of buildings of which the hotel consists, there was an open square paved with mosaic work, decorated with flowers, with a fountain placed in the middle, to render the place attractive during the summer months. Pianos and valuable paintings and sculpture were placed in the reception-rooms, to give an air of elegance, taste, and home comfort to the establishment. And for all these advantages of domestic comfort and rational enjoyment the charges were of a very moderate nature, *i. e.*, from four to five dollars, or less than a pound a week. It was intended to reduce the charge if in so doing the institution would continue to be self-supporting. The cost of erection was two millions of dollars, which was borne entirely by the original founder. This was an example of co-operative consumption of a very high order, which admits of imitation elsewhere, raising the standard of life, affording the means of literary and æsthetic culture, and creating a sense of comfort and pure enjoyment without degrading those benefited into the position of recipients of charity. Nor need it interfere with personal liberty, although, in every respect offering the advantages of Fourier's Phalanstère. Unfortunately, the strict rules of the hotel deterred the young women for whom it was erected from availing themselves of its benefits, and after a time it had to be given up as a philanthropic institution. It is now an ordinary hotel. But the failure of the scheme is not a reason for not trying it under more favourable circumstances, avoiding in future to interfere unnecessarily with the liberty and personal predilections of the inmates, who, though living by law, might be left to be as nearly as possible a law to themselves.

In a similar way, but on a still more practical principle, the attempt has been made by M. Godin, of Guise, to combine the advantages of industrial co-operation with domestic association in his arrangements for the division of profits in his trade, and the erection of the Phalanstère, or common domicile, for his workpeople.

According to M. Godin's plan of dividing profits, capital receives fifteen per cent. interest, the workman his usual wages, and a sum is set apart to defray the charges of administration, and to reward mechanical inventions. The remainder is allocated in the proportion of one-third to the reserve fund, and the remaining two-thirds to capital and labour, according to the fixed amounts payable to each from the earnings before the nett profits were ascertained. The practical operation of the system is thus illustrated by Sir Thomas Brassey, to whose work we are indebted for the details of M. Godin's system[1].

Assume that the sum payable had been,—

Wages	£9,000
Interest on £40,000 at 15 per cent.	6,000
General Wages	1,000
	£16,000

Then if £2,400 be the nett profit, one-third, or £800, equal to 5 per cent. on the fixed expenditure, is put to the reserve, and the balance £1,600 is appropriated to capital and labour, in proportion to their respective shares in the fixed earnings. Thus the sum of £900 is added to the earnings of the wage receivers, the sum

[1] "Lectures on the Labour Question," by Thomas Brassey, M.P., p. 148.

of £600 is payable as bonus to the capitalist, and £100 to the management. Under the system usually adopted, capital would have claimed the whole of £1,600.

Such a plan, in which the workmen recognise that their interests are identical with those of their employers, must produce more remunerative work, and will prevent strikes and other conflicts by which both parties are losers.

M. Godin also provides a " social palace" for his employés, which is capable of housing no less than nine hundred people, and contains a variety of rooms to suit the purses and tastes of each of the inmates. The building cost £40,000, and small shares are obtainable by workmen, who thus become joint owners of the building, and their own landlords. The rent of rooms yields a return of three per cent. The social palace at Guise stands in the midst of extensive and well-kept pleasure-grounds on the banks of the Oise. It has an excellent theatre, where dramatic representations and concerts are frequently given, by associations formed for the purpose by the operatives.

The internal management is carried on by committees, consisting of persons of both sexes, and the general moral tone of the community is said to be superior to that of people in the same position living in isolated households.

The supplies of fuel and food, the cooking and attendance, even the early nursing and care of children, are left to efficient persons appointed for that purpose at the charge of the whole community. The women, as the committee of management, supervise the quality of provisions supplied from the co-operative stores and butchers' shops connected with the place. They also attend to the management of children and the general arrangement of the household [1].

Here again we have the advantages of co-operative action in avoiding waste, while securing good quality, combined with domestic economy, also in extending the amount of leisure,—the work being done systematically instead of in the slovenly and irregular fashion too often seen in the isolated household. The Phalanstère surpasses the latter, on the pattern of which it is founded, in granting full liberty whilst yet maintaining a thorough system of organisation such as Fourier aimed at.

But such institutions, excellent as they are, may be considered too much in the nature of patronising beneficence on the part of the employer. That mode of combination which assumes more independence on the part of the employed is co-partnership between masters and

---

[1] Mr. Godin's services have been recently recognised, and he has received the Cross of the Legion of Honour.

men, of which there are many interesting
instances given in J. S. Mill's treatise on
" Political Economy[1]." We will extract one
example. " M. Leclaire, a Paris tradesman,
who employed on the average 200 workmen,
made the following experiment. After paying
the usual wages, and assigning for himself a
fixed sum for his labour and responsibility as
manager, besides a certain percentage of interest
on his capital, he divided the nett surplus profits
at the end of the year among all, himself included, in proportion to the earnings. This he
found to be the best way of securing good and
peaceable workmen. It gave stability to the
management of his establishment (housepaint-
ing), and so led to pecuniary success. Community of interest thus became the bond of
mutual goodwill, whilst the unusual punctuality
and activity of those employed, owing to this
fact, amply compensated the employer for the
sacrifice of profits incurred. Leclaire left a
fortune of £48,000, and had divided among his
men, individually and collectively, £44,000;
he constantly insisted that his conduct had been
for his own advantage, and that it was better
for him to earn a hundred francs and give fifty
of them to his workmen, than to earn only
twenty-five francs and keep them all for himself.

[1] Book iv. ch. viii. § 5 and ff., p. 461 *et seq.* (People's Ed.)

" I maintain," he wrote, in 1865, " that if I had remained in the beaten track of routine, I should not have arrived, *even by fraudulent means*, at a position comparable to that which I have made for myself."

Leclaire proved to his *own* satisfaction, that enlightened self-interest can be attained only by the path of self-sacrifice. The spring of all his actions is revealed in these words, which are contained in his will—" I believe in the God who has written in our hearts the law of duty, the law of progress, the law of sacrifice of one's-self for others. I am the humble disciple of Him who has told us to do unto others as we would have others do unto us, and to love our neighbour as ourselves. It is in this sense that I desire to remain a Christian unto my last breath."

He left directions to be buried with the same simplicity as the members of the Mutual Aid Society, and was followed to the grave by his six hundred workmen.

Thus Leclaire removed the antagonism between capital and labour, by converting the very antagonist into the bond of union between master and men ; by making the wealth created by labour the servant of all, blessing alike employer and employed.

Resting on a sure foundation, the " Maison Leclaire " grows each year more and more prosperous, so that, eight years after the death of its founder, the amount of business done was exactly doubled. The annexed table will show the share of profits paid over to the workers individually and collectively during the last five years; the figures bear sufficient evidence of the continued prosperity and vitality of the firm.

YEARS.	PARTICIPATION OF PROFITS.			WAGES.	Proportion of Profits to Wages Paid.
	Mutual Aid Society.	Bonus to Labour.	Total.		
	Frs.	*Frs.*	*Frs.*	*Frs.*	*Per cent.*
1842–76 inclusive	...	...	1,750,017		
1877	57,000	115,000	172,000	615,484	17. 81
1878	65,500	130,000	195,500	713,644	18.216
1879	80,000	160,000	240,000	867,870	18.435
1880	95,000	190,000	285,000	972,424	19. 53
1881	107,500	215,000	322,500	1,068,607	20. 11
			2,965,017		

It will be seen from the above, that the sum paid over in bonuses to the men amounted last year to £8,600, while the Mutual Aid Society was allotted £4,300 as its share of profits, the two managing partners jointly receiving the remaining quarter, *i.e.*, £4,300, as their share.

The whole amount paid over to the workers since 1842, when Leclaire first divided his £475 among his forty-four men, now reaches the considerable sum of £118,600 [1]. Others followed the example of M. Leclaire, and with equally signal success.

Sir T. Brassey, in the work already referred to, mentions some co-operative foundries established on a similar principle in New York and Massachusetts, the birthplace of so many unsuccessful Socialistic experiments. One of them was started in 1866 with a capital of £27,000 paid up. The shares were fixed at £20, and limited in number to 2,000. In the first year thirty-two men, in the second seventy-five, and in 1869 eighty-five men, were employed in the works. A dividend of 10 per cent. was made in the first year, and 30 per cent. more was paid on labour. The second year the dividends on stock and labour amounted to 89 per cent. In 1869 they reached 100 per cent. The most skilled trades earn, owing to their steady employment, 35 per cent. more than the same classes of workmen would earn at similar wages in a private foundry. This success is due to greater economy in the use of materials, and the superior discipline of the men at their work.

[1] See "A brief sketch of the 'Maison Leclaire,'" by Mary M. Hart (2nd thousand), from which the above is quoted by permission. Miss Hart and her friends have lately established a society in London called the "The Decorative Cooperators Association," to be carried on on the same principles. Mr. Albert Grey, M.P., is its President.

But we pass on to the highest form of collective enterprise, that in which the men have been entirely emancipated from the tutelage of the masters, and conduct business on their own account, with their own capital, and under the management of men chosen from among themselves. We know that this was the idea which inspired Louis Blanc, and to embody which he was induced to reserve certain governmental loans or grants to the working classes in 1848.

Then and since, private attempts were made in the same direction, which, beginning in a very humble way—often with only a few tools belonging to the founders, and small sums of money collected from their savings, or lent by other working people poorer than themselves— have issued in very fairly prosperous concerns. The success of many of them affords the best answer to the unfavourable predictions and misrepresentations of the opponents of the principle. The struggles of these pioneers of co-operation were of the most heroic nature, and frequently led to very remarkable results.

"Often," says M. Fengueray, in a sketch of their history quoted by Mill, "there was no money at all in hand, and no wages could be paid. The goods did not go off, the payments did not come in, bills could not get discounted, the warehouse of materials was empty; they had to submit to privation, to reduce all expenses to a minimum, to live sometimes on bread and water. . . . It is at the price of these hardships and anxieties that men who began with hardly any resource but their goodwill and their hands succeeded in creating customers, in acquiring credit, forming at last a joint capital, and thus founding associations whose futurity now seems to be assured."

Here is an example of one of these. It was proposed to establish a pianoforte manufactory, and to start it two delegates of several hundred workmen asked the Government, in 1848, for a subvention of 300,000 francs. The commission refused the grant, and the project was abandoned. But what happened? Fourteen workmen, the two foiled delegates among them, determined by themselves without either cash or credit to start the association. These fourteen men went to work with their tools, and each member with some difficulty contributed his share of ten francs as circulating capital. With the help of contributions from other working men not concerned but sympathising with the undertaking, the association was formed, their total stock amounting to near 2,294 francs. This was on March 10, 1849. Two months elapsed before any wages could be paid. They lived, as workmen out of employ live, sharing the bread of their comrades who happen to be at work, pawn-ing such articles as they possessed, and so forth. They executed a few orders, and received pay-ment on the 4th of May. With this they paid their debts, and after dividing the remainder into equal portions of five francs on account of wages, they agreed to devote it to a fraternal repast by way of commemorating this first victory in the co-operative campaign. For some time they struggled on against fearful odds, with a piece of good-luck now and then to encourage them. The result was that, when taking stock at the end of 1850, the number of shareholders had increased to thirty-two. Large warehouses and workshops, at the rental of 2000 francs, were no longer sufficient for the business, and the amount of their capital, after deducting all liabilities, was 3,293,002 francs. Later on they separated into two societies, one of which alone, in 1854, possessed a circulating capital of 56,000 francs (£2240), which had risen to £6520 in 1863.

Other associations having a similar history and boasting of like successes were founded, and sur-viving obloquy and opposition, are standing mo-numents of the cause, determined not only to ensure prosperity for themselves, but to promote the general adoption of co-operative principles by means of independent combination among the working classes.

From reports of British consuls in foreign countries, Sir Thomas Brassey quotes several promising cases in favour of co-operative production. In Sweden, we are told, the men willingly risked their savings for the sake of seizing an opportunity of rising from a dependent position to the freedom of co-operative industry. We shall have occasion in the next Chapter to show what progress the same movement has made in this country. We shall now briefly refer to the system adopted by Schulze Delitzsch, the great advocate of self-help, with a view of encouraging co-operative industry in Germany. In his practical efforts to improve the condition of the German labourer by this means, Schulze Delitzsch deserves the warmest commendation and unqualified respect from all those who take an interest in the subject. He is perhaps too much *doctrinaire* in his desire to establish the principle of self-help, but there can be no doubt as to the practical good done by credit banks, and the direct as well as indirect aid afforded to the spread of co-operation among the humbler classes of small shop-keepers and tradesmen, and the working classes generally.

Schulze Delitzsch is a man of legal training and habits, and for some time held government appointments until his liberal tendencies, too freely expressed in the Prussian Parliament, led to official persecution and irritating chicanery, which induced him at last to give up his appointment and devote himself entirely to the promotion of his pet schemes for the amelioration of the labourer's position. He commenced by establishing an association for the purpose of wholesale purchases of raw material, and also a credit bank, for the joint use of small tradesmen in his own town, Delitzsch (whence his cognomen, to distinguish him from others of the same name sitting in the Prussian Parliament). Later on, the principle of association was extended over a larger area, and was made to include not only credit banks and societies for the purpose of purchasing raw material and the acquisition of machinery, but also building societies, co-operative stores, and similar institutions, and was more or less under the direction of a central organisation with Schulze Delitzsch at the head. The results, up to the end of 1881, are given by Schulze Delitzsch in his last report, as follows. There are —

1889 credit associations, or national credit banks.

898 associations for procuring raw material, storing of manufactured articles in different industries, or engaging in productive enterprise.

660 co-operative stores for the distribution of
articles of consumption.

34 building societies.

As, however, some of the newly-formed
societies are not comprehended under this head,
Schulze Delitzsch estimates the whole number
of associations in the German Empire at 3500
to 3550, with a total of 1,100,000 to 1,200,000
members, possessing property of their own to
the amount of about nine-and-a-half millions
pounds sterling, and additional working capital
of twenty-one millions entrusted to the associations for investment by outside creditors.
It is surmised, however, that some of the members belong to a better class than those for
whom the association was intended, and that
that partly accounts for the large amount of
capital subscribed. Be this as it may, the main
credit arises from the fact that all the members
are depositors to some extent, and that all subscribers are responsible for the liabilities of the
associations. It is remarkable that the knowledge of this solidarity of interest has consider-
ably augmented the credit of these associations,
which has been good throughout, and has remained unshaken in years when a commercial
crisis threatened the existence and security of
the most trusted joint-stock companies in Germany. Schulze Delitzsch calculates that about

300,000 labouring people in one form or another share in the benefits of this system of co-operation [1].

An organ of the press represents the interests of the association, and there exists a public Association Bank, with a subscribed capital of a million sterling, in the capital of Germany, with branches elsewhere, to maintain intercourse with the business world outside. But all transactions between members and the association are carried on in the ordinary principles of trade and reciprocity: self-help, not benevolence, being the rule throughout. The profits are divided pro rata in proportion to the capital subscribed, and a large reserve fund is put aside yearly to provide for losses and fluctuations of trade. The number of members is unlimited, and resignation of membership is free to all by giving the notice customary on such occasions.

Referring to these associations, Mr. Holyoake, in one of those aphorisms which are often more incisive than explanatory, says: "The German co-operator sets up credit banks; the English co-operator sets up stores. The Germans lend money, the Englishman makes it [2]." There are

[1] The above figures have been corrected by Dr. Schulze Delitzsch, to whom and Dr. Schneider the author owes many thanks for the trouble they have taken in revision.

[2] "History of Co-operation," vol. ii. p. 99.

more credit banks in Germany because, owing to the peculiar economic condition of that country, trade and agriculture on a small scale are still struggling on, and have not yet reached the brink of hopeless extinction, as is the case in this country; and it is the small tradesman and small farmer whom Schulze Delitzsch thought in the first instance to benefit, and in so doing brought the labourer also within the magic circle of capitalistic enterprise. But if neither the one nor the other had been deserving of credit, the banks would have been soon shut up—for creditors in Germany as well as in England do not as a rule lend money without hope of repayment. The encroachment of large capital has been longer resisted by small industrial enterprise, and peasant proprietorship has struggled more successfully against the competition of *latifundia* in Germany than anywhere else, and hence the special need of philanthropic enterprise in aiding them in their unequal conflict. It is found that the most active and intelligent among those benefited by Schulze Delitzsch's institution join the productive associations pure and simple, and this is co-operation of the best kind. Here the labourers take the initiative to establish themselves as a new society, independent of the leadership of capital;

and Schulze Delitzsch acknowledges that the Socialistic agitation of the last twenty years had aided not a little this spirit of enterprise.

Upon the whole, as to the results of co-operation, its great originator in Germany is able to report progress along the entire line[1]. Among the tokens of success he mentions a fact which may serve as a lesson to English co-operative storekeepers, that several of the distributive associations set apart out of their proceeds a fund for educational and mental improvement purposes, the erection of educational establishments, such as technical schools to continue the training received in the primary schools, the erection of popular libraries, and the acquisition of landed property and buildings for the production on their own premises of many articles of consumption required by working men. In this way co-operation becomes a lever which raises those connected with it to a higher level, and enables them to participate more freely, not only in the material resources, but also in the intellectual wealth of the community.

The dearth of circulating capital among the peasant proprietors of Germany, which leaves them at the mercy of usurers and others who provide the small loans they require from time

---

[1] There are now 3481 associations of different kinds compared with 3250 in 1880.

to time, induced another philanthropist, M. Raiffeisen, formerly the burgomaster of Hammersfeld in Rhenish Prussia, to establish credit banks for farmers, of a similar though not identical nature to those established by Schulze Delitzsch mainly in favour of the manufacturing classes. Raiffeisen does not require any shares to be taken by those benefited by his loan associations. He however makes every member responsible, to the whole amount of his personal property, for the liabilities of the association to which he belongs, so as to secure not only credit from without, but also cautious dealing in the internal management of the affairs of the society, which are mainly entrusted to the most enlightened men of good position in the localities where the associations are formed. Money is advanced on personal security, which is sufficient in small villages where everybody is known, and misrepresentation and dishonest speculation are rare or impossible. The profits arising are not divided, but represent a reserve fund for future contingencies. The associations are, so to speak, mutual benefit societies to protect those concerned and their survivors from the danger of burdening the soil with heavy liabilities, and so endangering their present independence. They were not intended to be money-making concerns, and are based not so much on the principle of self-help as that of mutual Christian support. They are intended, as a warm advocate of the system says, to be a justifiable Communism resting on community of interests, adopted as the only means for the preservation of the impoverished peasant proprietor, to preserve him against the blandishments of the unjustifiable Communism of Socialistic agitators, having for their motto, " Similia cum similibus curantur."

The experiment thus far has been successful, and the credit of the association all that could be desired. In fact, there have been more offers of capital for investment than were required, which is easily accounted for when we remember that the landed and moveable property of every member of the society are sufficient security to cover all debts, especially as there are scarcely any expenses of management, which is left mostly to honorary officers. There are now about one hundred of these credit institutions. Some have existed for twenty-eight years, and have been favourably reported of by Professor Nasse, who was one of the members of the late enquiry instituted by Government as to the usefulness and security of these associations. The only danger in a society of this sort, as in the case of benefit societies in England, is the temptation to divide the profits. Hitherto the strong common-sense of the members and the

saving habits of the German farmers have preserved them from this temptation.   It is to be
hoped that their increasing prosperity will remove in course of time the necessity for the
existence of such a fund altogether, because no
loans will be required for carrying on the business of the persons concerned, as each will have
saved sufficient capital to dispense altogether
with an artificially created credit[1].

The general usefulness and prosperous condition of the various agricultural and industrial
co-operative associations, which have been
steadily increasing during the last thirty years
on the Continent, must inspire every sincere be-
liever in the cause with hope for the future success and extended influence of the movement.

In every new effort at confederate action
among the labouring class we see a further
promise of a peaceful solution of the labour
question, and a further step in the direction of
true international unity of peoples, in spite of
passing clouds of exclusive and selfish isolation
on the part of individuals and nations, which
obscure the gladdening prospect in the distant
horizon of a general confederation of mankind—
an *Associated Humanity.*

---

[1] Schulze Delitzsch calculates that the number of these
agricultural associations at the present moment is from 600
to 700.

CHAPTER XI.

COLLEGES OF INDUSTRY.

" THE silent revolution of industry, produced
by the rise of co-operative devices, will
save England from the plague of State Socialism." Such is the deliberate statement in a
short but weighty article on State Socialism
from the pen of a veteran in the ranks of co-
operators—Mr. Holyoake. Nor is it at all
unlikely that by the extension of the principles of co-operation and self-help, the emancipation of labour from the power of capital
will be effected peaceably, and in the course of
natural evolution in this country, just as its
liberal institutions have grown and strength-
ened without the convulsive efforts of revolutions such as have accompanied social and
political changes elsewhere. This being the
probable destiny of the co-operative movement,
it is all the more interesting to follow its course
from its origin to the practical or constructive

stage in which we find it at present, so as to be able to venture upon a forecast as to its possible future, its prospective goal. Even so cautious a writer as Professor Fawcett has not hesitated in expressing a conviction that "co-operation may probably be more confidentially relied upon than any other economic agency to effect a marked and permanent improvement in the social and industrial condition of the country."

In the early pioneer movement, from 1812 to 1844, the heroic age of co-operation, many and various were the attempts of philanthropists and patronising employers to improve the condition of the working people. One experiment after another was made,—as for example those of Robert Owen,—but all ended, as most social experiments are apt to do, in comparative disappointment, and some in abrupt failure.

That general uneasiness of society which periodically manifests itself, and demands that something should be done to restore the body politic to health and comfort, made itself specially felt during this period in the various attempts at political reform and the widespread desire among social philanthropists to substitute a social system based on co-operation for the existing competitive one, so as to give the toiler a larger share in the results of his labour.

A long-forgotten ancient form of social life, that of association, was remembered at a time when society was suffering from the excesses of individualism. It was thought that a return to this more simple mode of life would remove those social evils which prevailed at the time, just as a return to the principles of protection at the present moment is advocated by those who are dissatisfied with the unprosperous condition of trade in the country. To secure equality it was thought best to fall back upon the more ancient forms of industrial co-operation, and to organise labour more or less on the Communistic plan. This attempt proved a failure, for to go back is a vicious principle in social economy. But the experiments, though unsuccessful, led the way to the more healthy form of co-operation of independent labourers without patronage— " a scheme of voluntary equality," as it was called by Mr. Pare, an enlightened pioneer of co-operation.

One of the earliest instances of co-operative stores was the village shop, opened in the year 1794, at Mongewell, in Oxfordshire, to provide the families of the poor of that and some adjoining parishes with the ordinary articles of consumption at wholesale prices. It had been set up by Bishop Barrington, who seems to have understood the principles of co-operation tolerably well, but whose example appears not to have found many imitators among the bishops and clergy of that day.

"Colleges of Industry" had been recommended a century earlier by the Socialist co-operator, John Bellers. Long afterwards the so-called "Christian Socialists," Maurice, Kingsley, and Thomas Hughes, made a practical attempt to organise a system of associated labour of this kind in the metropolis, and with comparative success.

About the same time an attempt was made to create self-supporting villages by a number of noblemen and gentlemen, joined by a few of the bishops, who said in their prospectus that "Competition, in appealing to selfish motives only, enriching the few and impoverishing the many, is a false and unchristian principle, engendering a spirit of envy and rivalry." The same document held out a prospect of a time coming when, by means of these philanthropic efforts, the inhabitants would become proprietors of the villages so founded.

In addition to these, there were numerous pretentious schemes set on foot, such as the Orbiston Community, founded by Abraham Combe, in Scotland, and the more successful experiment of Mr. Vandeleur among the wild peasantry of Ralahine, in Ireland, both of which were founded on the pattern, and more or less in conformity with the principles, of Robert Owen's settlements.

Also belonging to this " enthusiastic period " was the Chartist Co-operative Farm scheme, which promised " a beautiful cottage and four acres, with thirty pounds to work it, for a prepayment of five pounds four shillings." It allured seventy thousand persons into member-ship, though it had only a subscribed capital of thirty-six thousand pounds, whereas it was cal-culated that no less than twenty-one millions would be required for the purpose.

The Queenwood experiment was a similar attempt, during this mythical age in the history of co-operation, to improve the condition of the people by adapting the principles of asso-ciation to the requirements of modern times. A book might be written on the " Idiots of Pro-gress," says Mr. Holyoake, referring to these and like experiments. Those of our readers who wish to study more minutely the " pic-turesque insanity" of these Utopian reformers, we can only refer to the pages of his highly interesting, and sometimes even humourous, " History of Co-operation."

We can do no more than allude to the viru-lent opposition which the movement encountered during this eventful period, and the imputa-

tions and unjust obloquy to which its early
heroes were exposed, when in some cases
clergymen refused to bury co-operators, and
" in one case a sexton caught the postumous
contagion, and refused to dig a grave for a
Socialist's child." The progress of the movement,
thus hampered by opposition, was slow and inter-
mittent. Its principles, not always clearly understood by its most prominent advocates, were
invariably disparaged by powerful enemies, and
misinterpreted by the outside world. Therefore all honour is due to those disinterested men
who, at the risk of their own reputation and
fortune, pursued undaunted their mission of
social reform, and so became the courageous
harbingers of social progress. They have paved
the way for their more practical and more
cautious followers. " The pioneers," says Holyoake, "who have gone have, like Marco Polo,
or Columbus, or Sir Walter Raleigh, explored,
so to speak, unknown seas of industry, have
made maps of their paths and records of their
soundings. We know where the hidden rocks
of enterprise lie, and the shoals and whirlpools
of discord and disunity. We know what vor-
tices to avoid."

The early co-operative movement collapsed
after thirty years of "valorous vicissitudes." But
it was found, after all, that co-operation was a

living principle, only suffering from "suspended animation." It revived under a more practical form, destined to meet with signal success. Its constructive character manifests itself in three successive stages: first, in the joint-stock company, then in the industrial co-partnership, which leads the way to the third and highest form of co-operation—combination among the labourers themselves. With the first of these we have nothing to do here. The second is still in its infancy in England, and the wide gulf which exists between wealth and poverty, and which produces a more marked class-separation of employer and employed than is desirable, holds out little promise of rapid progress so long as the ignorant suspicion of the sturdy labourer, proud of his pauperised independence, blinds him to the advantages of industrial co-partnership between himself and his employers. Progress is also hindered by the too frequent forgetfulness of the employer that partnership, not patronage, is the one thing needful to establish a healthy and peaceable, as well as profitable, co-operation between capitalist and labourer. Still, this form of co-partnership has and will continue to become more general as its benefits are shown by the attempts now being made at industrial co-operation among the men themselves. We have seen an instance of this in the last chapter,

R

where M. Leclaire adopted the principle, with marked success, in Paris.

We shall now allude to an English enterprise of a similar nature. Messrs. Briggs, of the Whitwood and Methley Collieries, near Normanton in Yorkshire, issued a proposal some years ago to "officials and operatives employed in the concern," to take up among them one third of the capital employed in their business in preference shares. When the profits on capital exceeded ten per cent. it was agreed that the surplus should be divided in two equal portions, one to go to the employer, the other to be distributed among the employed in proportion to their earnings during the year ; and the programme put forth at the time declared that "the adoption of the mode of appropriation thus recommended would, it is believed, add so great an element of success to the undertaking as to increase rather than diminish the dividend to the shareholders."

Nor were the promoters disappointed in this expectation. While it lasted the partnership with the labourers brought them great gain, and several thousands of pounds were divided among the workmen as their share of the profits. But unfortunately Messrs. Briggs, acting too much in the spirit of patrons, in contravention of the partnership principle laid down by themselves, refused to pay the promised dividend to any of their people who should attend the trades unions, and so hampered the proper working of their well-meaning scheme by unwarranted prescriptions and irritating dictation. This was unjustifiable interference with the liberty of the employed persons, and led to the inference that the company found strikes less expensive than fulfilling the conditions of a mutually advantageous partnership. The association was terminated by the employers without explanation, except that the company found it difficult to work the scheme satisfactorily in the presence of so many conflicting claims, interests, and prejudices. The more probable explanation is the employers' own general unfamiliarity with co-operative principles. They deserve credit, however, for what they attempted. They would probably have been successful if they had persevered, and made the participation in profits on the part of the workers less a gracious gift depending on the goodwill of the masters than a deservedly-earned remuneration for services rendered.

There have been also several attempts at co-partnership in agriculture, such as that of Lord George Manners, Earl Spencer, and the present Speaker of the House of Commons, which have not yet any telling results to show, owing to the backward condition of the agricultural labourer, and the present unfortunate depression of agriculture. But there is one remarkable case of co-operative farming which deserves to be mentioned as a successful experiment. Some forty years ago, a Suffolk landowner, Mr. Gurdon, when a small farm of his became vacant, called together twenty labourers, and offered to lend them capital without interest for the purposes of co-operative farming under his own direction. They agreed willingly to carry out the scheme. Ten years later they were able to repay the loan. He let another farm of 150 acres on the same terms to thirty more labourers, and in 1862 they had nearly repaid the capital, and all were living in a prosperous condition. From a report sent in to Mr. Holyoake by a gentleman who is by no means favourable to this plan of patronising agricultural co-operation, and whose testimony is therefore all the more valuable, it appears that the experiment of Mr. Gurdon, of Assington, *as far as it went*, has been certainly successful.

As to the advantages of industrial and agricultural co-partnership in promoting good feeling between employers and employed, in giving a direct interest in the concern to the latter, and in greater energy, skill, and economy in production, there can be no question. But its chief merit consists in serving as a school for productive co-operation among the men themselves, and the independent effort of labourers to form themselves into co-operative societies without the aid of patrons [1]. The distinction between the two has been tersely put by Mr. Holyoake : " In an industrial partnership capital employs labour. In a co-operative workshop labour employs capital." The employment of capital borrowed at the usual rate of interest of course depends on the public credit enjoyed by the association. This brings us to what Germans would call the " epoch-making " event in the history of constructive co-operation—the establishment of the stores of Equitable Pioneers at Rochdale.

This was, in the first place, simply a " scheme of shopkeeping for the working people, where no credit is given or received, where pure articles of just measure are sold at market prices, and the profits accumulated for the purchasers." The abuses connected with distribution, which doubled the price of commodities under which the labouring people were mainly supplied, led to this. Equity in industrial pursuits was their

---

[1] Victor Böhmert, director of the Statistical Bureau for the kingdom of Saxony, has shown, in a work lately published on the labour question, that in 120 practical cases of different industries, spread over various countries, the application of this principle has had the desirable effect of improving the social condition of the wages labourer and his relations with his employer.

object, as the name implies. Since competition failed to secure it, co-operation was resorted to as securing at once probity and prosperity in the commercial enterprise, and an equitable share of profit among all concerned.

The original capital of the society was collected by means of weekly twopenny subscriptions from the working men, who have since been called the "famous twenty-eight" Pioneers. With the sum of £28 so obtained, a small store was opened in Toad Lane, Rochdale, in 1844, for the sale of ordinary articles of consumption. Carefulness and honesty procured customers, additional subscribers, and a rapidly-growing business. This enabled the Pioneers to invest largely in shares of a co-operative corn-mill in 1855, which may be called the first experiment of co-operative production in this country. In 1857 the Equitable Pioneers' Society had its seven departments of grocery, drapery, butchering, shoemaking, clogging, tailoring, and wholesale. Since then it has still further expanded into branch stores, spreading its network all over the country. The acquisition of the co-operative corn-mill was followed by the formation of co-operative associations for cotton and woollen manufactures in 1868, and the definition of co-operation was now changed with the altered circumstances of the association. " The main principle of co-operation is that in all new enterprises, whether of trades or manufacture, the profits shall be distributed in equitable proportions among all engaged in creating it." In thus following out the principle of co-operation to its legitimate logical consequences, the Pioneers of Rochdale have attained unrivalled success in their enterprise. The store, which commenced with a small stock of goods, value £16 11s. 11d., has now been transformed into one of most extensive warehouses in the country, with its newsroom rivalling that of a London club, an extensive library, science classes and scientific apparatus, with an educational fund, set apart from the proceeds of the business, for the diffusion of literary culture among the members of the association.

By taking the public into partnership, and dividing the profits among producers and consumers, the Co-operative Association has made the rapid progress which is implied in the following figures :—

Years.	Members.	Funds.	Business.	Profits & Interest.
		£	£	£
1844	28	28	—	—
1854	900	7,172	33,364	1,763
1864	4,747	62,105	174,937	22,717
1874	7,639	192,814	298,888	40,679
1879	10,427	288,634	270,070	49,751
1880	10,613	292,570	283,655	48,545
1881	10,697	302,150	272,142	46,242
1882	10,894	315,243	274,627	47,608

In the year 1882 the profits and interest together of the Rochdale Equitable Pioneers' Society amounted to £47,608.

Nor are the Rochdale Stores singular in their startling success. The Halifax Society, which has a history of its own, was founded in 1829, under very humble circumstances, clearing in nett profits from 1830–32 the sum total of £173 2s. 11¼d. It has now 6762 or more members, with a yearly profit of £15,816; and, says Mr. Holyoake, with pardonable pride, "If it happens to lose £60,000, still goes on its way, no more disturbed than one of the planets when an eccentric comet loses its tail."

The co-operative societies throughout Lancashire manfully weathered the storm during the years of the cotton famine[1], and, according to Mr. Milner Gibson's parliamentary returns, it appears that their number at that time increased to 454, all of which were in full operation in the third year of the famine. The profits of 381 of them—excluding 73 societies which made no returns—were £213,600 during that crisis. This result is sufficient to prove the practical soundness of the co-operative principle,

[1] So, too, the co-operative societies on the Continent emerged unscathed from the unfavourable effects of the Franco-Prussian war and the commercial crash which followed in Germany.

and to secure for Co-operation a position of its own as one of the most powerful social forces in the country, and as having the promise of still further extension in the future.

What distinguishes the scheme from any of those previously mentioned is its self-supporting character. It is a self-managing scheme of the labouring people, organising themselves into a body of independent co-operators without aid from either public or private patrons.

The organisation received its completion in the formation of the Co-operative Wholesale Society, which has now several productive works, and was originally founded to supply the various articles of consumption required for distribution by the stores, and which, owing to the opposition of "the trade," it was sometimes difficult to procure on equitable or indeed any terms from the wholesale trade. The foundation of this great auxiliary of the co-operative movement was, therefore, a further step in the establishment of a federal alliance between producers and consumers. It was formed in this way. At a conference of delegates from industrial and provident co-operative societies, held in Oldham on the 25th October, 1862, it was resolved, "That all co-operative societies be requested to contribute *one farthing* per member to meet the expenses that may

arise in carrying out the resolutions of the conference." A statement of the probable benefits
arising from the establishment of a wholesale
depôt and general agency was put forward by
Mr. Greenwood, and the co-operators set to
work to call this agency into existence. Although it began its career at a most unfavourable time, its success from the first was satisfactory, and twelve months after its commencement Lord Brougham spoke in highly favourable
terms of its importance with respect to the
future development of co-operation. His predictions have been fully verified by the subsequent history of this "farthing federation."

The following table indicates the progress of
" the Wholesale " up to the present year :—

Year.	No. of Members in Societies who areShareholders.	Capital, Share, and Loan.	Value of Goods sold.	Nett Profit.
		£	£	£
1864	18,337	2,456	51,858	267
1867	57,443	24,208	255,779	3,452
1877	273,351	414,462	2,791,477	33,274
1882	403,784	613,003	2,904,980	35,734[1]

Such have been the results of modern co-
operation in this country ; and still greater results may be expected in the future. "If all the

---

[1] The above refers to England and Wales only. There is
a separate Scotch Wholesale at Glasgow, which was founded
in 1868, and which at the close of 1881 had a capital of shares
and loans of £126,814, and did a business of £986,646, with
profits amounting to £22,981.

societies were federated together," says Mr. Holyoake, "they might buy vessels, farms, and grazing
grounds, and set up *countless manufactories*, and
guarantee orders which would keep all profitably
going, secure good provisions and honest workmanship, and *add the profits of production* to the
profits of distribution among all concerned [1]."

Sanguine expectations are entertained of the
good time coming when these Associations will
grow their own agricultural produce on their own
land, and when they will import tea, coffee, and
sugar in their own ships from their own plantations, and an ambitious scheme has already been
seriously entertained for the promotion of international co-operation between England and
America.

Unfortunately, the progress of co-operation
is constantly impeded by ignorance and disregard of its principles among co-operators themselves. Even in the workshops of the "Wholesale," and in the Oldham cotton-mills, division of
profits among all the employed labourers does

[1] This notion, however, is founded on the mistaken idea
that the consumption of manufactures by the mass of the
population corresponds to this consumption of food, which is
very far from being the case.

The author is indebted to Mr. E. Vansittart Neale, the
General Secretary of the Co-operative Union, for this correc-
tion, as also for the kind revision of the foregoing statistics
and other valuable suggestions on the subject of the present
chapter.

not take place according to true co-operative
principles.   The shareholders in co-operative
concerns, though they be labourers themselves,
are as liable to become dividend-hunters as
other capitalists.   They engage their "hands"
on the usual terms, and are tempted to violate
the principle of co-operation in not allowing
them a share in the profits.   Even the Manufacturing Society of Rochdale, at times, was re-
luctant to surrender a share of the profits among
its labourers instead of adhering to the original
principle of the institution—*the common interest
of all the workers in the work*—which led to
the just censure of John Stuart Mill.   These
errors, however, must be expected in new forms
of industry struggling into existence, and can
with difficulty be got rid of, even after the system
has reached its full development.   As in the case
of industrial partnership, so too in co-operative,
it will be felt before long that to secure the
utmost amount of efficiency the best plan is to
allot to labour a share in the profits, setting aside
a fund year by year, in prosperous times, to provide for contingent losses, reverses and fluctuations of trade, which may be calculated as
recurring at given intervals.   It will be found
that the "cold and covetous" plan of carrying on
industry, whether in the ordinary or the co-
operative system, is by no means the most profit-

able, and that honesty in the surrender of a liberal portion of the profits in such cases is, after all, the best policy. Co-operative associations adopting a different method sail under false colours, and become untrue to their own principles, just as the co-operative distributive stores in London, such as the Civil Service Supply and others, are only inferior imitations and spurious adjuncts of the movement. These having discovered the benefits arising from co-operation in cheapening articles of consumption by economy in distribution, establish stores like those at Rochdale, but without any regard to the moral and social aspects of co-operation. There is no community of interest among managers, shareholders, and consumers. It amounts to nothing more or less than amateur shopkeeping among the higher classes, with the view of obtaining the necessaries and luxuries of life at a cheaper rate. But even thus they perform an important function in making the advantages of co-operation more generally known, as well as the benefits of the ready-money system, and their success, as far as it goes, assists the spread of true co-operative principles by enlisting public interest and sympathy.

The number of co-operative societies in England and Wales, according to the last report, published in 1882, was 1056; that of members

526,686, with a share capital of £5,806,545. The amount of money realised in goods sold was £20,129,217.   The nett profits as stated in the report were £1,145,218, to which £200,000 may be added by a rough calculation of imperfect returns, etc.[1]

This is a remarkable achievement compared with the failures of all previous schemes of social improvement.   It has gained for the system accordingly public support from influential quarters.   At the annual congresses held during the last ten years, some of the most eminent statesmen and political economists have occupied the president's chair, and the proceedings on these occasions have been of a most encouraging nature.   The importance of the movement is being generally recognised, and competent judges, not at all inclined to Utopian dreams, speak hopefully of its future as a great social lever for the improvement of the masses and bringing about reconciliation between capital and labour.

Such being the case, the questions we have to ask ourselves are these: Are we entitled to regard co-operation, with one of its early promoters, Dr. King, as " the unknown object which the benevolent part of mankind have always been in search

---

[1] See Report presented at the Fourteenth Annual Congress, 1882, pp. 93–97.

of for the improvement of their fellow-creatures?"
Has the search after the philosopher's stone in
Utopian alchemy led to the discovery of true
principles of chemical affinities and combinations
in the social world? Is a widely-extended and
fully-developed system of co-operation regarded
as a scheme of social improvement likely to be
ultimately successful in removing the social evils
which accompany the existing system? In
other words, is co-operation destined to displace
competition in the organisation of society,
in tending to a general competency among
all? Will it remove class differences and class
antagonisms which are a constant danger to
social peace? Is it within the power of co-
operation, as some of its advocates assert, to
substitute for greedy individualism a desire for
the social well-being of all, and to put in the
place of egotistical acquisitiveness the altruistic
principle of social duty? Is co-operation the
power which shall turn—

> " The vast machine
> Of sleepless labour, 'mid whose dizzy wheels
> The power least prized is that which thinks and feels,"

into an instrument increasing the material and
spiritual wealth of the many as well as the few,
so that all linked together by the federal ties of
common interests may work intelligently and
unitedly for the common good?

To answer these weighty questions we must understand the true nature and tendencies of co-operation. We must be able to show that the co-operative principle in its practical application avoids all those dangers on which other social schemes have made shipwreck, and supplies all those elements of success in which they were wanting. If this be so, co-operation would realise the socialistic ideal which has haunted the mind of man for ages without adopting the extreme measures proposed by socialism for its attainment.

" The two wants of industry," says a distinguished co-operator, " are distribution of profit and education in industrial morality." Co-operation supplies both, and when " distribution shall undo excess, the baser incentives to greed, fraud, and violence will cease. . . . We are but in that state yet, but co-operation is the most likely thing apparent to accelerate the march of it." If this be so we have gone far towards solving the social question.

On the material benefits of co-operation in the distribution of profit we have dwelt sufficiently long already. Of the educational tendencies, moral and mental—the spiritual forces of the movement, so to speak—it remains for us now to speak. The moral qualities most needed are frugality, liberality, and fidelity, to ensure saving habits and the creation of capital, as well as fair arrangements in the distribution of labour and profit. It was the absence of this "moral method of frugality" which led to the failure of most of the North American settlements we have described. On the other hand, co-operation, as an educational agency for teaching thrifty habits[1], has already achieved startling results in the progress it has made towards the abolition of a ruinous credit-system, and in accumulating vast capital among people who but a few years ago were without any means whatever, so as to render shares in co-operative associations, both at home and abroad, the most secure investment of the times.

"It is only a liberal frame of mind among men that can make a co-operative shop possible," says Mr. Holyoake. The absence of liberality

[1] It has been asserted that the co-operative store proving the chief attraction to the labourer, encourages with increased cheapness a larger desire for consumption, and is thus opposed to frugality. It is forgotten that the standard of living among the labourers is still generally very low, and that a wider diffusion of comforts among them is far more desirable than simply increasing the luxuries of the few who are now in full enjoyment of the "wealth of nations." Moreover, it has to be remembered that the chief cause of brutalising self-indulgence has been the unhealthy anxiety for overproduction since the rise of modern industry, and the desire of immediate gratification on the part of those whom the stupefying effects of machinery-labour render insensible to the more rational enjoyments of ideal culture. When the labourer, by

proved fatal to some of the Communistic societies we have described, whereas those co-operative
institutions where it prevailed have prospered
most.   It is the true principle of co-operation,
and without it the hard cruelties of competition
will only be reintroduced by a back-door in
co-operative concerns.   But where the principle
viribus unitis prevails among persons engaged
in the same pursuit, all participating alike in the
results, the amenities of federal union will not
be wanting.

The Hon. Auberon Herbert, M.P., speaking
at the Birmingham Congress of 1871, alluded
to "the fidelity and moral *passion*" which
should characterise co-operators.   Now the distrust of the working class towards their own
members is proverbial; a distrust, alas! too
often founded on sad experience.   It was this
mutual distrust which led to the break up
of many of the communities in Europe and
North America.   But what are the real tendencies of co-operation in this matter?   They
are comprehended in the following preamble to
the rules of the Co-operative Union, adopted at
the London Congress in 1875: "This union is

means of co-operation, shall have become a capitalist, he will
not only have learned sobriety and frugal habits, but also the
art of living a higher life than his present animal existence,
and he will equal in refinement and taste his by no means
too far advanced employers.

formed to promote the practice of *truthfulness, justice,* and economy in production and exchange."

Co-operation thus helps in the formation of character; it dignifies labour in rendering the labourer independent. The introduction of the " gaseous " element, which destroyed the Communistic societies founded by Robert Owen, is a danger which co-operators avoid. The discipline of co-operative labour has no attraction for the rabble, and for those who join its ranks in a depraved condition it is the best school for the reformation of character.

Mental aptitude, next to moral force, is an important element in society. Its absence was painfully felt by the originators of the North American Phalanxes. Co-operation, apart from teaching its members wholesome lessons on the functions of capital, and removing many erroneous impressions as to its relative importance compared with labour, aims also at providing technical and general education, and at creating a taste for higher enjoyments in literary culture and æsthetic tastes. This will eventually produce self-respect in the working man, and make him conscious of his position as a member of the " order of industry " whose mission it is to " subjugate nature and turn the dreams of thought into realities of life," whose place in that proud army of conquerors that brings matter under the dominion of mind makes him the pioneer of progress marching in the vanguard of modern civilisation.

Co-operation realises the ideal of an " industrial army," and every co-operative society is an industrial phalanx as superior to those conceptions of Fourier, so crudely practised by American Socialists, as in its military disposition a modern Prussian regiment directed by a Moltke surpasses the Macedonian phalanx in the pre-scientific era of warfare under the generals of Alexander.

Discipline and order are the pre-requisites of efficiency in an army. They are more easily maintained among intelligent and self-governing bodies of men than among the ignorant and the unruly, the servile crowd and the craven slave. Co-operation implies self-discipline and the power of self-government, superior intelligence and organised independence, and therefore avoids the danger of disorganised conflict in the competitive struggle on the one hand, and the over-organising tendencies of Socialistic systems on the other.

Good officers and superior leadership are next in importance to the industrial army. The want of the " right kind of genius to guide " proved fatal again and again in the social experiments made on former occasions. The tendency also of good leaders to consult their own interests in the conduct of affairs rather than the welfare of the community has been a constant danger even in co-operative enterprises. In the present system of competition, administrative skill is secured simply by the survival of the fittest, and self-interest is the best security for good management. How are these to be obtained in co-operative societies? In the same way, we reply, as the governing heads in constitutional states, who are chosen by the suffrage of their fellow-labourers, with the additional aid of the educational advantages afforded by the co-operative process. First-rate ability in the management of business is rare, hence we have many cases of failure in the present state of things, resulting from errors of judgment committed by directors and other responsible heads of firms. In co-operation, as in competition, these dangers exist, but the popular form of government prevailing under the former proves a safeguard against hasty speculation and reckless over-production, especially when, in a long course of training, the members of the co-operative council find able supporters in their followers in directing the movements of the industrial army.

But union of the whole body, union of action

and union of sentiment, are indispensable to
victory. Discord, sooner or later, undermined
all the North American associations, one of
which, called the "One Mention Community,"
only proved true to its appellation after all
the members but one had departed from the
settlement after the dissolution of the society.

Fourier's dream that " two or three thousand
discordant centrifugal individuals in one great
house would fall by natural gravitation into a
balance of passions, and realise a harmony,"
must prove eventually impossible, and so it
was found when the experiment was tried even
on a smaller scale. But co-operation, setting
out with a less ambitious programme, aims
at union among a few at first, who gradually
increase. It is a union founded primarily on
self-interest, a union for creating and dividing
profits among all engaged. But it is more :
co-operation stands on a higher moral platform.
It not only attempts to "cancel competition
within its own range of action, and thus mitigate
its presence ;" it not only "surpasses the present
system, in which union of self-interest even is
not consciously present in the violent struggle
of all to promote their own individual good, but
co-operation aims at fraternal equality, by means
of equitable association, to procure a moderate
competence for all, and so removing the gulf

between extreme wealth and indigence, which renders the poverty of the many sharper and more abject by the side of the splendid, ever-growing, bewildering, masterful, and aggressive opulence of the few, which menaces by endowing dreadful anarchy itself with the charm of change."

These are the main principles and tendencies of co-operation. All that is required is true enthusiasm to make co-operation the great social power of the future. Hitherto there has been no want of enthusiasm, energy, or perseverance on the part of this little army of pioneers. They have endured hardship as soldiers in a great cause, struggling against innumerable obstacles. Some of its famous promoters, in the earlier days of the movement, set to work with almost religious zeal to spread its doctrines, taking for their motto, " Men, ye are brethren." The cause has had its martyrs too, especially in the camp of the "Christian Socialists[1]." It would be well if the true religious fervour which inspired the early pioneers still continued to animate its present promulgators, religious fervour without the sectarian spirit which led to internal dissensions in former experiments, as opposed to irreligious indifference which proved fatal to Robert Owen's scheme. Religion would

[1] See Holyoake, " History of Co-operation," ii. p. 395.

aid the cause as a regenerative influence in the
character of the individual, imparting the moral
force required for co-operative effort.   Religion
is too, as Guizot remarks, a great "associative
power" to bind together the members of the
Co-operative Union in the bond of Christian
love, taking for their watchword the Biblical
phrase, " And they helped every one his neighbour, and every one said to his brother, Be of
good cheer."

72399